CW01597252

EYEWITNESS QUICK STARTS

VOLCANO

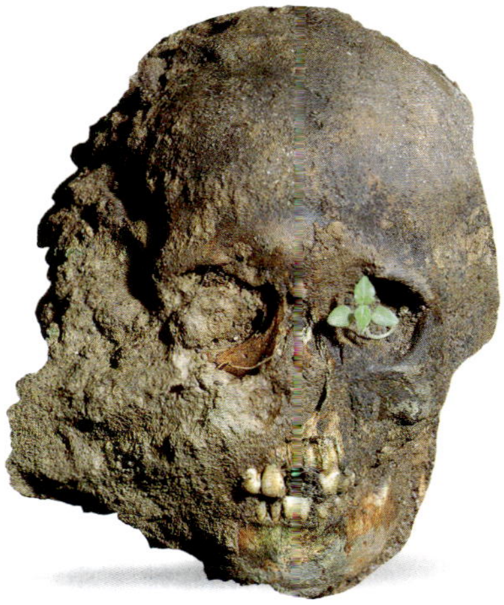

◀ Skull from Herculaneum

▲ Lava bomb

▲ Sulphur

▲ Seismograph from 1885

◀ Bread from Pompeii

◀ Cut peridot

▲ Olivine

Cut and uncut diamond ▼

▲ Walnuts from Pompeii

◀ Eggs from Pompeii

Body cast from Pompeii ▲

▲ Strands of lava

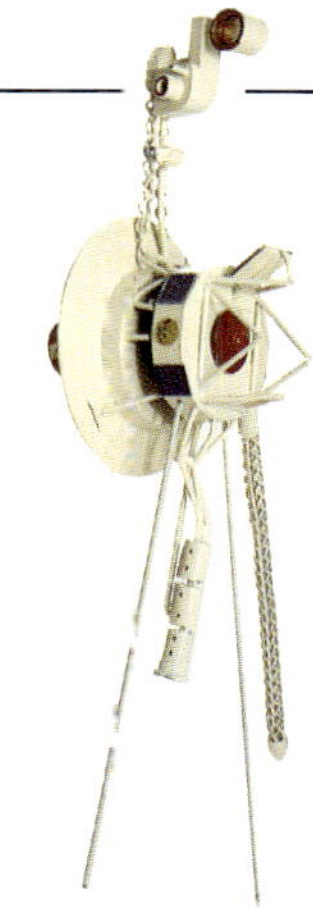

Voyager ▲ One

EYEWITNESS QUICK STARTS

VOLCANO

Written by

ROSIE NELSON

▲ Melted bottle

▲ Melted perfume bottle

◀ An ancient Chinese earthquake detector

DK

DORLING KINDERSLEY
London • New York • Moscow • Sydney

▲ Seneca, a Roman who wrote about earthquakes

◀ An ancient book about volcanoes

Melted fork ▲

Melted pocket ▼ watch

▼ Instrument for mapping the ground

◀ Lava stalagmite

A DORLING KINDERSLEY BOOK

Senior Editor Susan Peach
Managing Editor Jane Yorke
Senior Art Editor Marcus James
DTP Designer Almudena Díaz
Production Lisa Moss
Picture Research Kathy Lockley
Special Photography James Stevenson
Volcano Consultant Keith Lye
Reading Consultant Cliff Moon

This Eyewitness ™ Guide has been conceived by Dorling Kindersley Limited and Editions Gallimard

This book is based on *Eyewitness Volcano* by Susanna Van Rose, published by Dorling Kindersley Limited. The original text has been simplified.

Published in Great Britain by Dorling Kindersley Limited 9 Henrietta Street, London, WC2E 8PS

2 4 6 8 10 9 7 5 3

Copyright © 1992, 1998 Dorling Kindersley Limited, London

Visit us on the World Wide Web at http://www.dk.com

All rights reserved. No part of this publication may be reproduced, stored in a retrieval system, or transmitted in any form or by any means, electronic, mechanical, photocopying, recording, or otherwise, without the prior written permission of the copyright owner.

A CIP catalogue record for this book is available from the British Library.

ISBN: 0-7513-6125-9

Colour reproduction by Colourscan, Singapore
Printed in Singapore by Toppan

Statue of ▶ Zhang Heng

Contents

▲ Brown agate

Unstable Earth

Volcanic eruptions and earthquakes happen when nature gets out of control. Magma is melted rock which is found inside the Earth. Sometimes magma pushes up to the surface. This can result in volcanic eruptions, earthquakes, and geysers.

▲ **Cone-shaped volcano**
Some volcanoes are cone-shaped. Others are broad and flat. Most volcanoes lie deep beneath the sea.

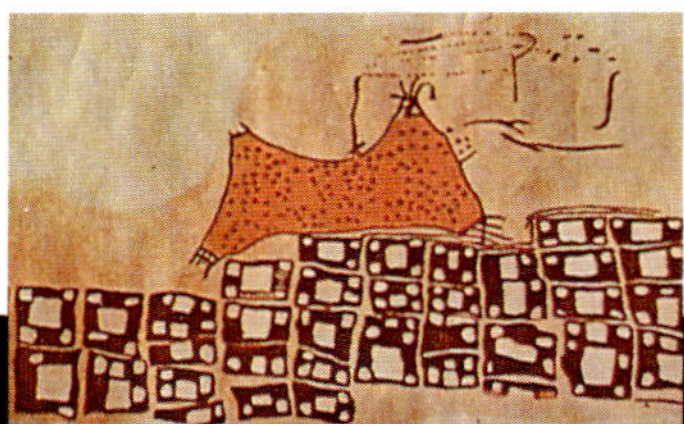

◀ Ancient painting of a volcano erupting

▼ **Erupting volcano**
When a volcano erupts, red-hot rock (lava) pours out of a hole in the Earth.

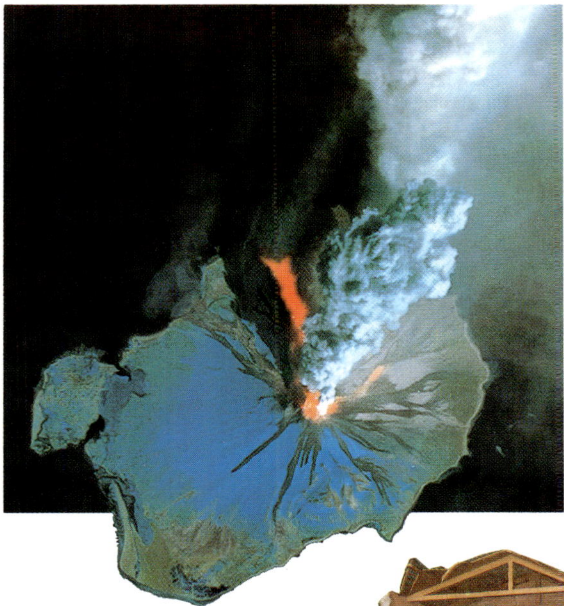

◀ Some people think that warm volcanic sand can cure diseases.

◀ **Seen from space**
An erupting volcano sends clouds of ash high into the sky.

▲ Geysers are hot water springs heated by magma.

▲ **Earthquake damage**
This 600-year-old Italian painting shows the scene after an earthquake.

▲ **San Francisco, 1989**
In 1989, an earthquake shook San Francisco, USA. Many buildings collapsed and 62 people died.

Below the surface

If you could go on a journey to the centre of the Earth, you would soon get very hot! We live on the thin skin, or crust, of the Earth. Below that lies a layer of very hot, mostly solid rock called the mantle. Sometimes the rocks in the mantle get so hot that they melt. This melted rock is called magma.

▲ **Hot as hell** Some people used to believe hell was a hot place below the Earth's surface.

Inside the Earth? ▶ Old pictures like this one show how people once thought volcanoes worked.

The ocean floors are made from a heavy rock called basalt. ▼

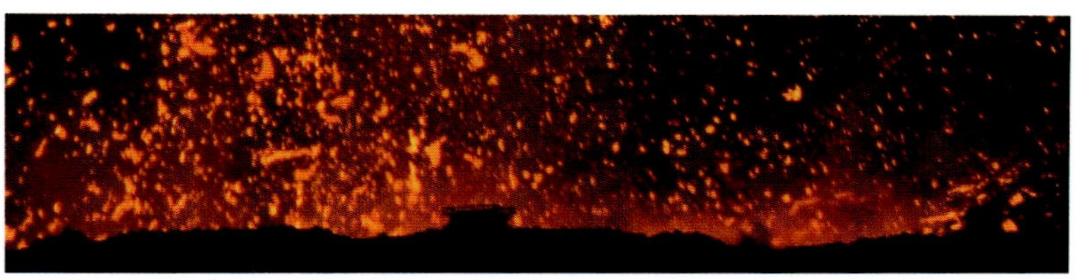

▲ Liquid rock shoots out of a volcano.

If the Earth was the size of an apple, the Earth's crust would be no thicker than the apple's skin. ▶

▲ In Jules Verne's book *Journey to the Centre of the Earth*, the heroes climb inside a volcano.

Land is ▶ made from lighter rocks such as granite.

◀ Iron melts when it reaches 1,535° Celsius. Most of the Earth's core is hotter than this.

◀ Iron meteorites come from the cores of other planets. They show us what the Earth's core is like.

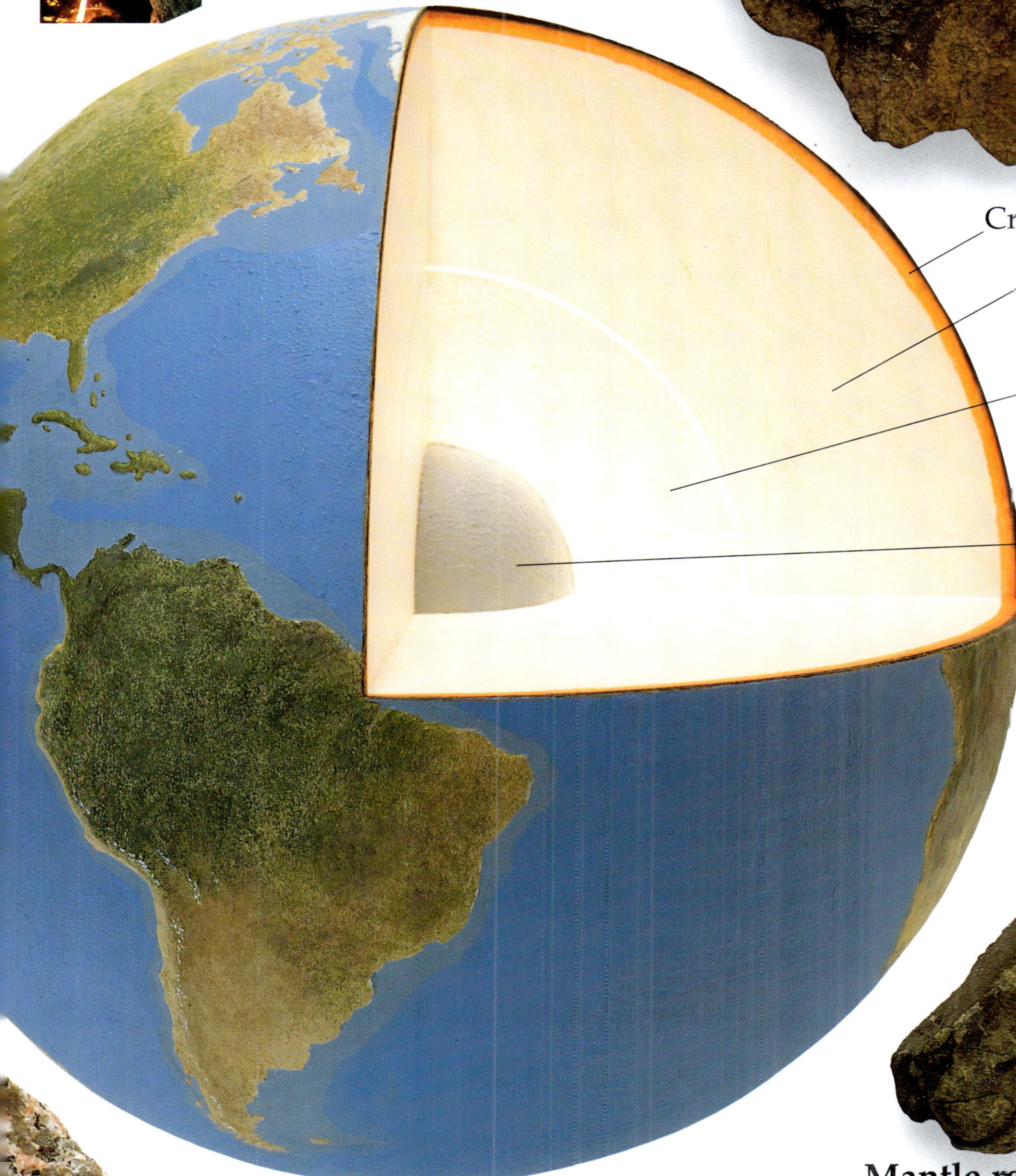

▲ **Layers of the Earth**
The surface of the Earth is the cool crust. Beneath the crust lies the mantle, which is mostly solid rock. Beneath the mantle is the metal core.

Mantle rocks ▲
Sometimes magma carries bits of the mantle to the surface.

The Earth's crust

Ancient Greeks and Romans thought the god Atlas carried the world on his shoulders. ▶

Volcanoes and earthquakes are more common in some places than in others. This is because the Earth's hard, outer layers are broken into large pieces, called plates. These plates fit together like odd-shaped paving stones and they are constantly moving. Volcanoes and earthquakes happen where two plates meet.

Moving continents ▼
The German scientist, Alfred Wegener, believed that the world's continents had once been joined together but had slowly moved apart. He called this movement "continental drift".

▲ Pink areas on this map show where earthquakes are most likely to happen. The black triangles are volcanoes.

A plaster cast of a man who died in a volcanic eruption in Italy in AD 79.

This crack opened up in the ground after an earthquake in Japan, in 1925.

The plates exposed
This model shows the Earth with no water in the oceans. The brown ridges are the edges of some of the plates.

Coloured plates
This globe has been coloured to show how some of the plates fit together.

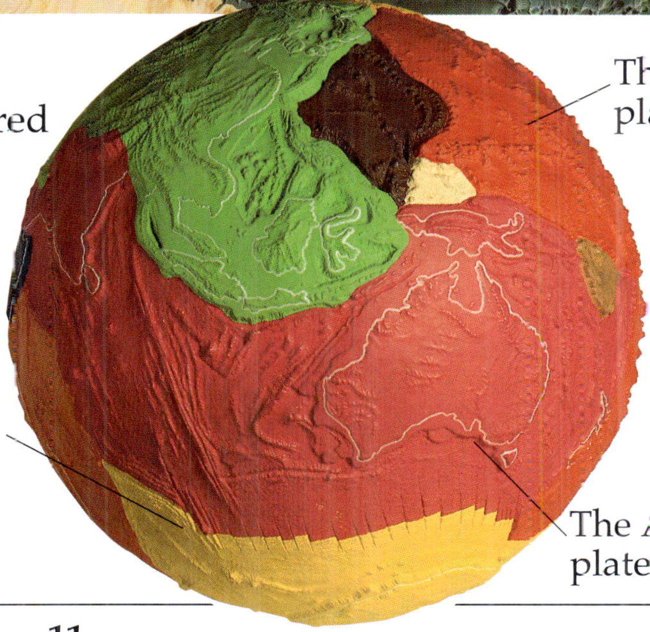

Mount Erebus is a volcano in Antarctica.

Moving plates

When two plates collide, one plate is forced down beneath the other plate. This is called a subduction zone. When two plates move apart, a spreading ridge is formed.

Iceland lies ▶ across a spreading ridge. The island is made almost entirely from volcanic rock.

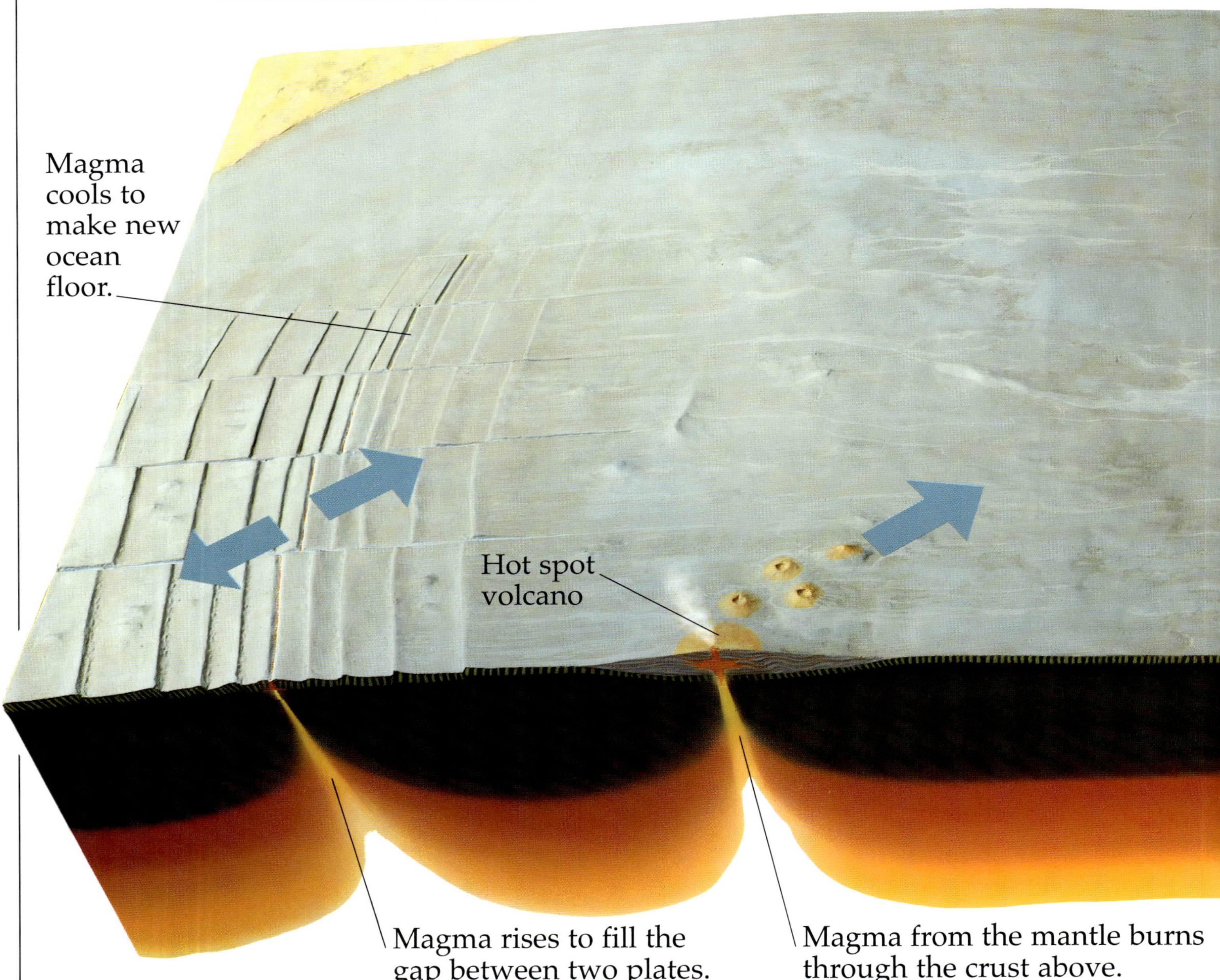

▲ **Spreading ridge**
New ocean floor is formed where two plates are pulling apart. Magma rises up and hardens to fill the gap between the plates.

▲ **Hot spot**
In some places, volcanoes are found in the middle of a plate. These are called hot spots.

◀ This chain of volcanoes in Guatemala, Central America is caused by a subduction zone.

The San Andreas ▶ fault in California, USA is caused by two plates sliding sideways against each other.

A deep ocean trench where one plate sinks below another.

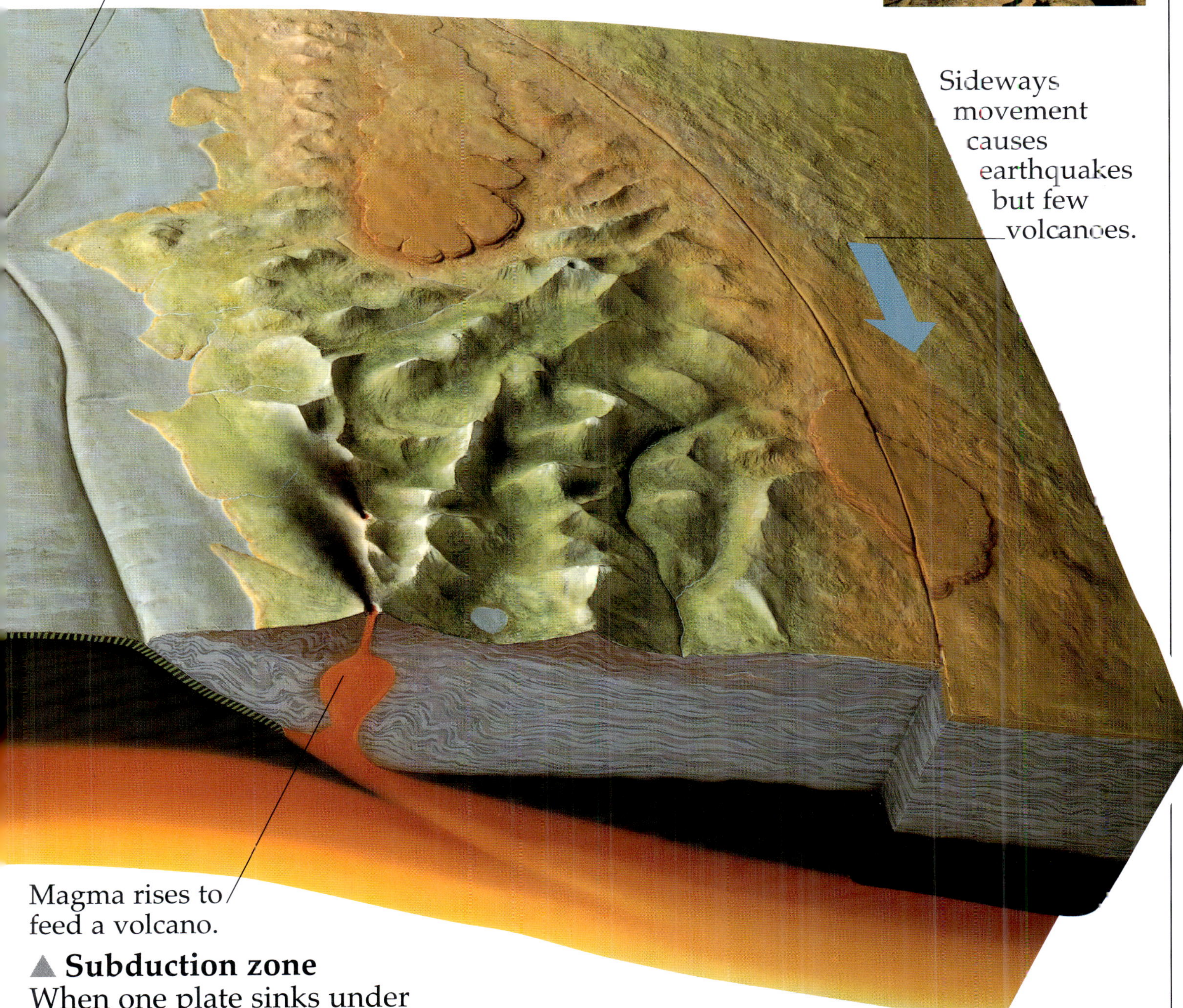

Sideways movement causes earthquakes but few volcanoes.

Magma rises to feed a volcano.

▲ Subduction zone
When one plate sinks under another, there are earthquakes and the crust melts and turns to magma. This magma rises to feed volcanoes.

▲ Rubbing sideways
When two plates move alongside each other, they cause earthquakes.

Mount St Helens

▲ Mount St Helens before the eruption

Volcanoes that are constantly erupting are called active volcanoes. Those that lie quiet for hundreds of years are called dormant volcanoes. However, when a dormant volcano does burst into life, the eruption can be violent. This happened to a volcano called Mount St Helens, in northwest USA. It had not erupted for 123 years but, on 18 May 1980, it exploded killing 57 people. The explosion lasted for nine hours and was heard 320 kilometres away.

▲ **38 seconds after the explosion**
For two months, there had been small eruptions on Mount St Helens. Then, on 18 May, the north side of the mountain exploded.

▲ **Magma reservoir**
Magma built up beneath the volcano in an underground pool, called the magma reservoir.

▲ **42 seconds after**
Ash and rock poured down the side of the mountain. A cloud of ash began to rise into the air.

Ash cloud ▶
A photographer took this picture of the eruption just before he ran to his car. The cloud of ash and mud chased him as he drove to safety.

▲ **Sticky lava**
For several years, magma continued to rise up the feeder pipe. It oozed out at the top of the volcano as thick, sticky lava.

▲ The eruption destroyed everything near the volcano, including trees up to 50 metres tall.

53 seconds after ▶
There was a huge ash cloud. Rocks were thrown into the air.

Ash and dust

▲ Pieces of lava

When a volcano erupts with a big explosion, clouds of ash pour into the sky. This happens because there is a lot of gas trapped in the magma. As the magma escapes from the volcano as lava, the gas explodes and blasts the hot rock into pieces of ash and dust.

▲ Pieces of ash

▲ Volcanic dust

▼ Cone-shaped volcanoes
When lumps of lava, ash, and dust explode out of a volcano, they often pile up around the volcano to form a cone shape. This is called a cinder cone.

History of a volcano ▶
Each time a volcano erupts, the ash falls and cools to make a new layer of rock. Each layer in this rock shows when a new eruption took place.

◀ An ancient ash flow in Italy

Glowing avalanche
If the cloud of ash rising from a volcano is heavy, it sometimes collapses and flows down the sides of the volcano. This is called a glowing avalanche.

▲ **Buried in ash**
In June 1991, Mount Pinatubo in the Philippine Islands erupted. A huge cloud of ash rose into the sky, blocking out the sun for many days.

◀ Farmers led their buffaloes out of fields buried in ash.

▼ **Dusty crops**
The ash from Mount Pinatubo covered crops in a thick layer of dust.

▲ A wet cloth helps to keep the dust out of your lungs.

Lava

Red-hot lava is sometimes runny and trickles from a hole in the ground. Sometimes it is thicker and explodes into the air. Runny lava runs down the side of the volcano like a glowing river. This is called a lava flow. Eventually, lava cools and turns back into solid rock.

◀ **Heated lava**
This lava block frothed when it was reheated by scientists. It still contained a lot of gas.

Lava bomb from ▶ Mount Etna

Round lava ▶ bomb

▲ **Lava bombs**
Gases trapped inside the lava send rocks called bombs or blocks flying into the air.

Lava exploding ▶ from Mount Etna in Sicily, Italy.

Lava block with ▲ a twisted tail

◀ A flow of aa lava in Hawaii, USA. Some of the lava is red-hot and glowing. Some is cold and black.

◀ Rope-like pahoehoe lava

▲ As pahoehoe lava begins to cool, a wrinkled skin forms on its surface.

▲ Aa and pahoehoe
There are two kinds of lava flow. Aa (pronounced "ah-ah") lava is sharp and scratchy. Pahoehoe ("pa-hoy-hoy") lava is smoother.

Smooth, folded lava from a pahoehoe flow ▼

▲ The sharp lava in an aa flow is called scoria.

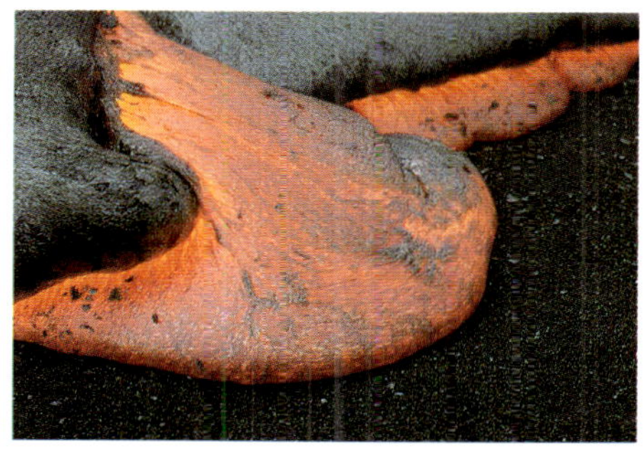

▲ Pahoehoe flow
Hot lava breaks through the skin of a pahoehoe flow. This is how the lava creeps forward.

Black volcanic sand ▼

Black sand ▶
When red-hot lava flows into the cold sea, the lava shatters into tiny pieces of volcanic sand.

Gas and lightning

▲ Characters in a *Tintin* story flee from smelly volcanic gases.

Volcanic gases can be very dangerous. In 1986, an explosion released a cloud of poisonous gases from Lake Nyos in Cameroon, Central Africa. The cloud rolled over nearby villages and killed 1,700 people. The main gas in the cloud was carbon dioxide, which has no smell. However, many other volcanic gases are very smelly!

▲ **Smelly gas**
Volcanoes give off a gas called sulphur dioxide that smells of rotten eggs.

Steam clouds
In 1963, an eruption near Iceland formed a new island called Surtsey. As sea water met hot magma it turned into a cloud of steam. ▶

▼ **Gas mask**
If you go near an erupting volcano, you must wear a gas mask for protection against gas and dust.

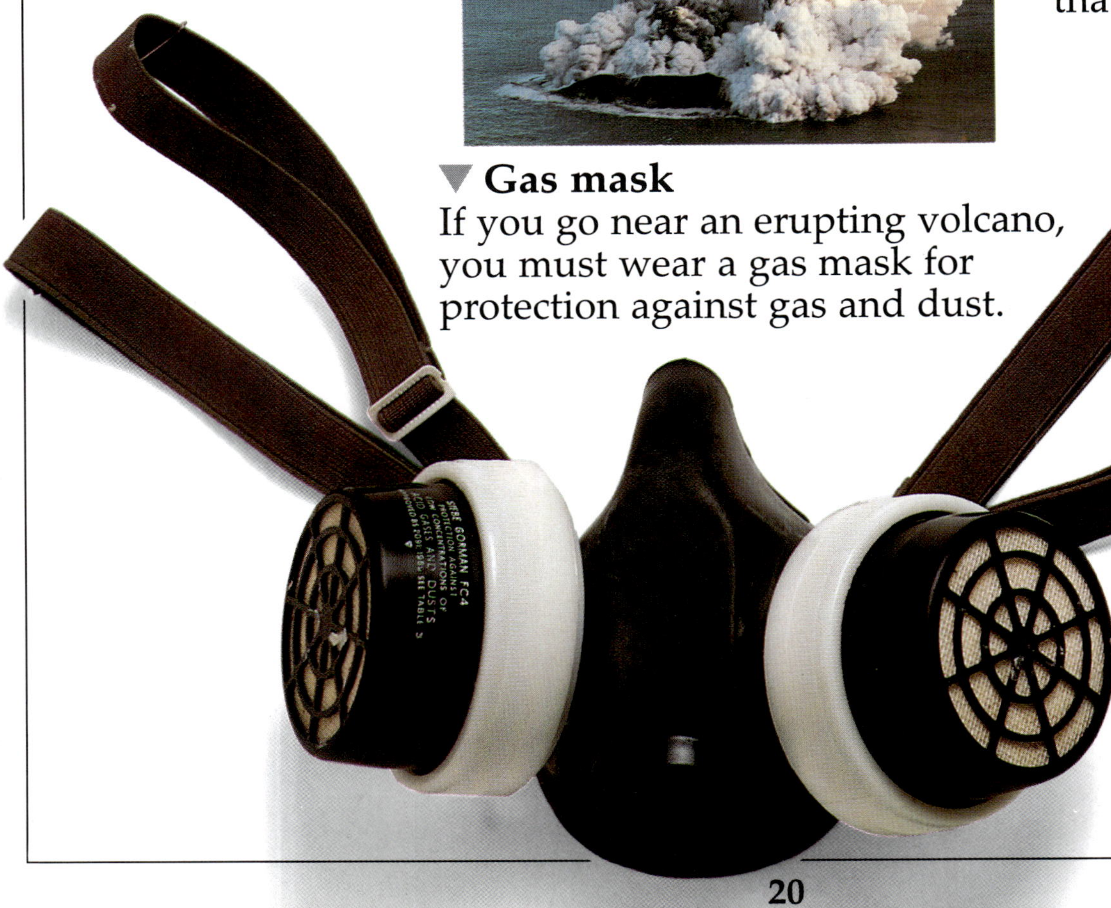

Scientist wearing ▼ a gas mask

◀ **Lightning**
There are often lightning flashes during an eruption. This picture of lightning in Siberia was taken during the day!

◀ When Mount Vesuvius in Italy erupted in 1779, there were lightning flashes.

▲ **Scientists test acid water**
This lake in the volcano Kawah Idjen, in Indonesia, is full of volcanic gases. The acid water would burn human skin in minutes.

Pumice is a ▶ kind of lava. It is very light because it is full of gas bubbles.

Hot spots

In some areas of the world, the mantle is very active and makes a lot of magma. A hot spot is where this magma manages to break through the Earth's crust above. As the plate moves across the hot spot, the magma forms a chain of volcanoes. Some of the biggest volcanoes on Earth lie over hot spots.

Goddess Pele ▲
Some people on Hawaii believe that the goddess Pele makes the mountains, melts the rocks, and builds new islands.

▼ Mauna Loa erupts
One of the world's biggest volcanoes, Mauna Loa, lies on the Pacific island of Hawaii, USA. The Hawaiian islands are a chain of hot spot volcanoes.

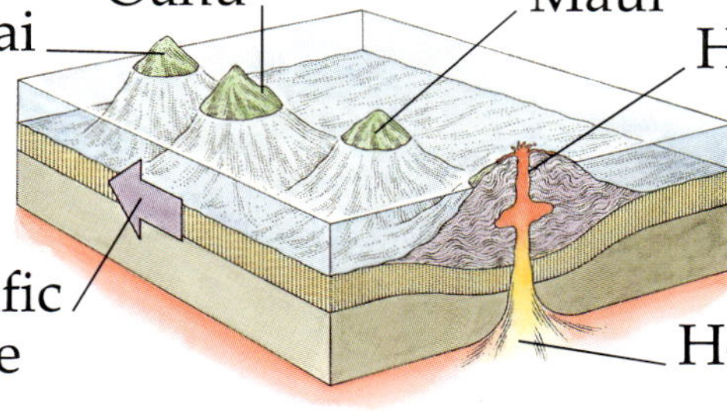

Volcanic islands ▲
There is a hot spot underneath the Pacific Ocean. As the Pacific plate moves across the hot spot, magma erupts to form a chain of islands.

▲ These fine threads of lava are called Pele's hair.

Hot tip ▶
This eruption is on the island of Réunion in the Indian Ocean. The island is the tip of a hot spot volcano which rises seven kilometres above the ocean floor.

Stalactite of lava from a lava tube ▼

▲ **Lava tube**
Sometimes pahoehoe lava forms a skin that is thick enough to walk on. Beneath the hard skin, hot lava still flows in a tunnel, or tube.

▲ Lava has cooled and hardened around this tree.

◀ A road on Hawaii, buried in lava

Lava in a tube stays hot and can travel many kilometres, destroying fields and villages. ▶

Spreading ridges

Places on the ocean floor where two plates are moving apart are called spreading ridges. As the plates move, volcanic eruptions constantly make new crust to fill the gap. The lava erupts quite gently because of the great weight of water pressing down on it. The lava makes rounded shapes, called pillow lava.

▲ **Ridge through Iceland**
In Iceland, you can see a spreading ridge on land. This ridge began to form in 1783.

▼ **Ocean floor volcano**
This huge volcano lies 4,000 metres below the surface of the Pacific Ocean.

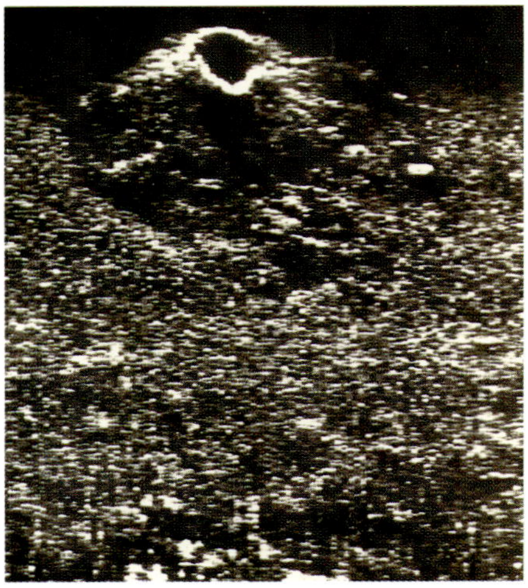

▼ This submersible is used to take photos of spreading ridges underwater.

▲ In Iceland, eruptions are often from long cracks in the ground.

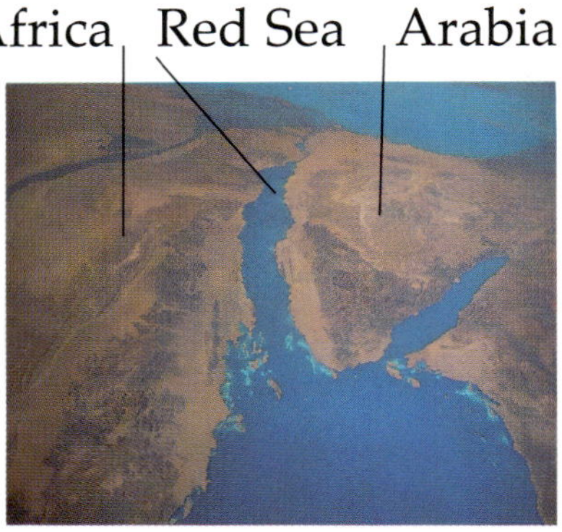

◀ There is a spreading ridge under the Red Sea. This means that Arabia is moving away from Africa.

◀ These rare prawns live near black smokers in the Pacific Ocean.

Black smokers ▶
In some places along spreading ridges there are hot springs, called black smokers. The water that pours out of them is coloured black by minerals.

Tube worms around black smokers in the Pacific Ocean.

▲ These urchins feed off the minerals in the hot water around black smokers.

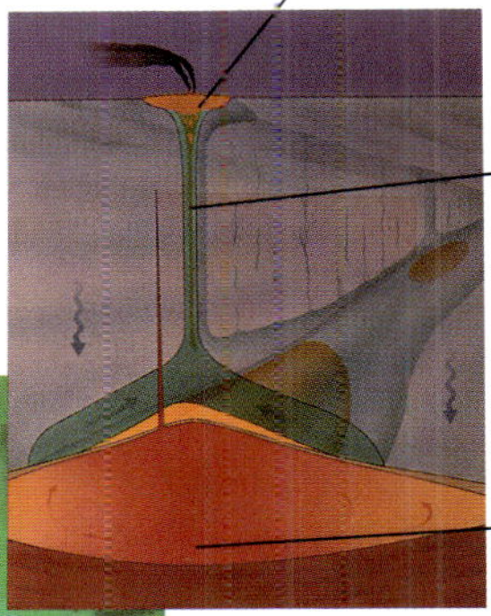

▲ The water of a black smoker is heated by a reservoir of magma below.

◀ **Chimneys**
When minerals from a hot black smoker meet the cold ocean water, they become solid and form chimneys.

▲ Pillow lava

These rocks from the ▲ ocean floor contain the metal manganese.

▲ There are scars from two feeder pipes on this rock.

▲ Gabbro is a rock formed in magma reservoirs.

Mount Vesuvius

▲ The Roman writer, Pliny, saw Mount Vesuvius erupt.

Mount Vesuvius is a volcano near Naples, in southern Italy. It's most famous eruption was on 24 August AD 79. Ash and stones from the eruption buried the Roman towns of Pompeii and Herculaneum. The towns lay forgotten for hundreds of years. Then, in the 1700s, people began to dig up the buried buildings and objects.

These maps show where Vesuvius is in Italy.

Ash cloud

Everyday life ▼
The people of Herculaneum and Pompeii were busy doing everyday things like baking bread when Vesuvius erupted.

A loaf from ▶ Pompeii

Part of a floor ▲ mosaic from Pompeii

A flour mill made from lava ▼

◀ A modern Italian loaf

▲ Picture from a floor mosaic

▲ A bowl of eggs from Pompeii

Lots of gold and silver ▲ jewellery was found in Pompeii. This snake bracelet is made of gold.

▼ Fresh walnuts

◀ Fresh figs

Carbonised food
This food contained carbon and did not burn in the heat. Instead, it just turned into charcoal.

◀ A bowl of figs, found at Pompeii

▲ A bowl of walnuts from Pompeii

▲ This is a painting of what Pompeii looked like when Vesuvius erupted.

Pliny's letters ▶
In his letters, Pliny described how his uncle tried to rescue people but died from breathing dust and gases from the volcano.

Body casts

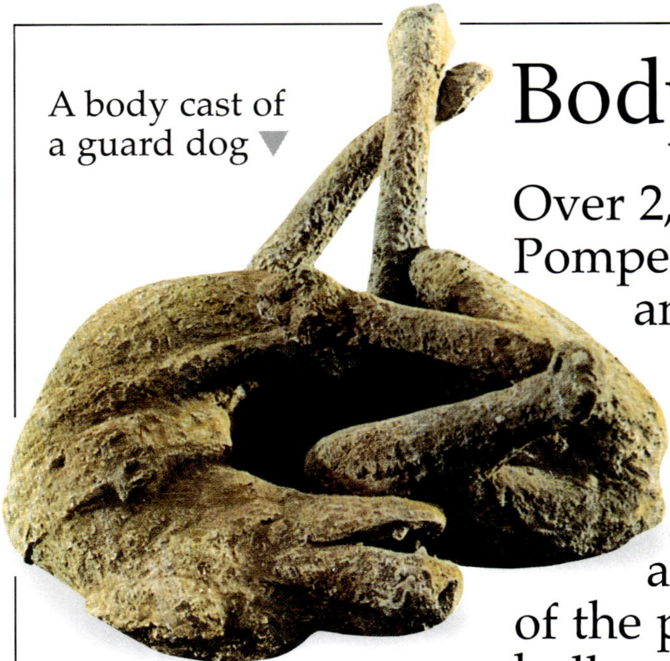

A body cast of a guard dog ▼

Over 2,000 people died in Pompeii from breathing in ash and dust. As they fell, ash and lava covered their bodies. Slowly, the lava hardened and the bodies rotted away. But the shapes of the people were left as hollows in the rock.

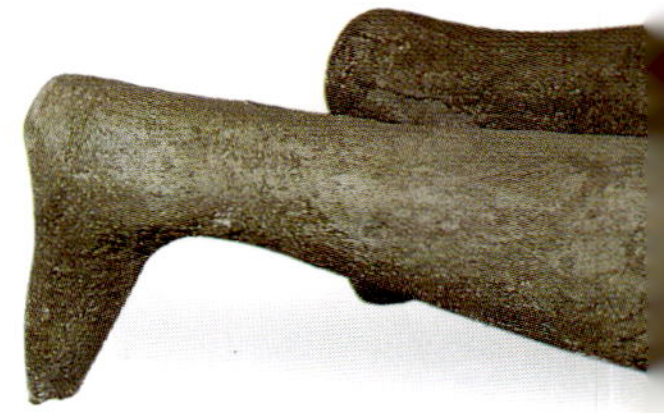

1

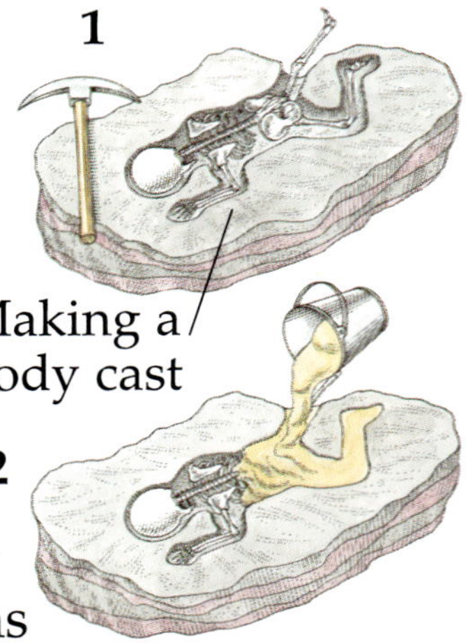

2

Making a body cast

Body casts ▶
During excavations in 1860, Guiseppe Fiorelli invented a way to make casts of the Pompeii victims using plaster of Paris.

▲ This painting shows the end of Pompeii. It is by the German artist, Karl Bruillov.

▲ Plaster of Paris set around a baby's skeleton

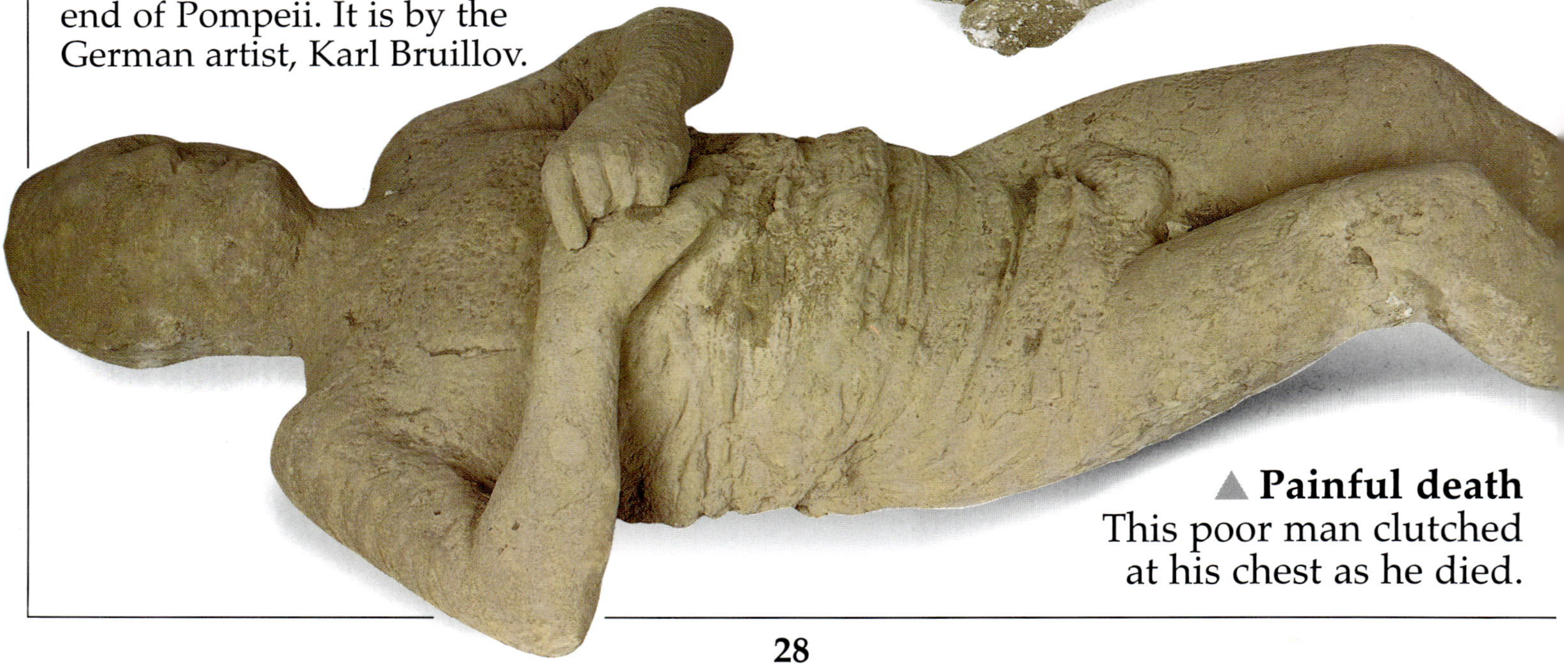

▲ **Painful death**
This poor man clutched at his chest as he died.

This man covered his face as he died.

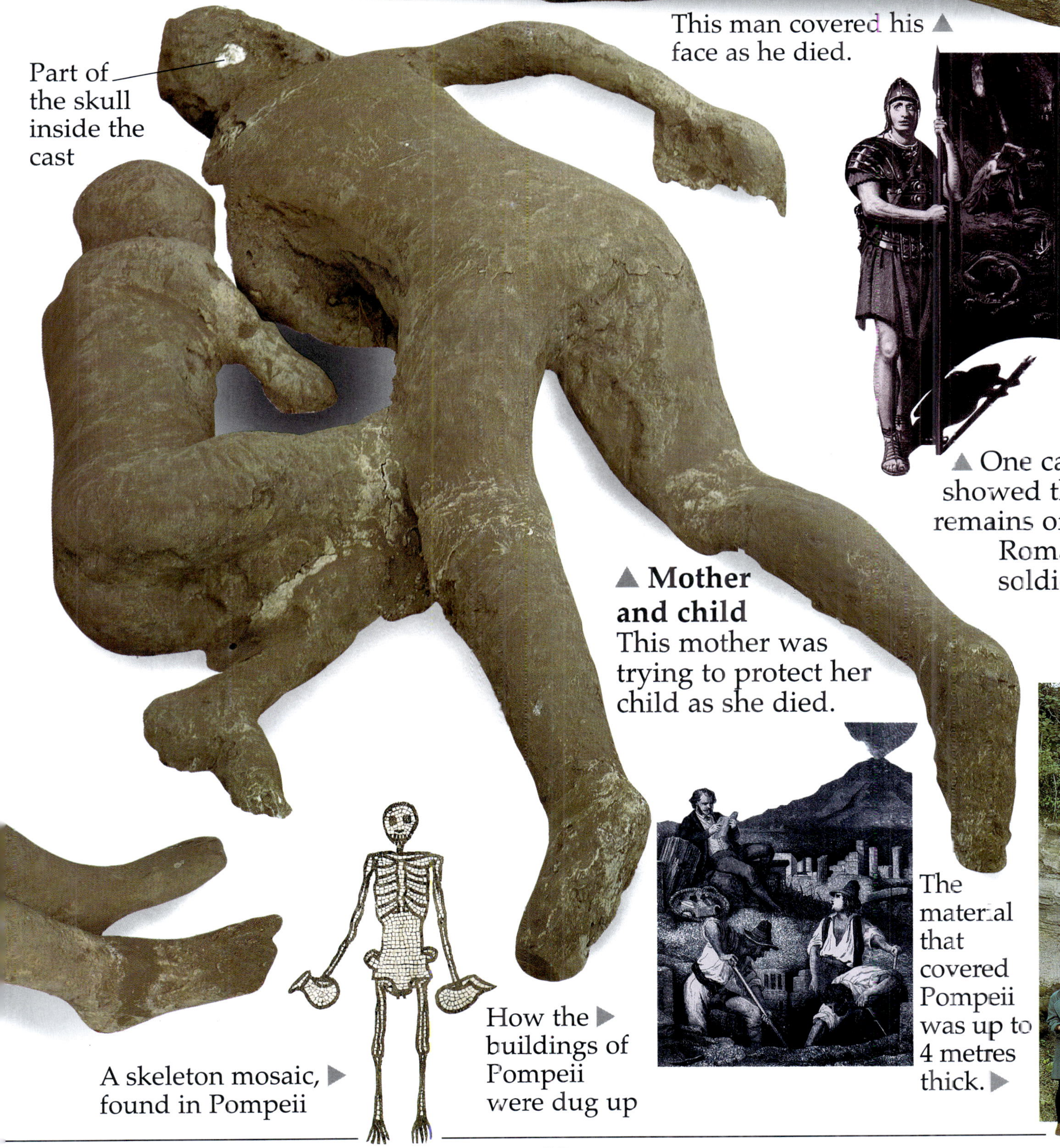

Part of the skull inside the cast

Mother and child
This mother was trying to protect her child as she died.

One cast showed the remains of a Roman soldier.

A skeleton mosaic, found in Pompeii

How the buildings of Pompeii were dug up

The material that covered Pompeii was up to 4 metres thick.

Herculaneum

When Vesuvius erupted, a huge flow of ash and rock also covered the town of Herculaneum. But many people had time to escape this disaster.

▲ Remains of a skeleton from Herculaneum

▲ A mosaic from a house in Herculaneum

▲ Today, you can walk through the ruins of Herculaneum and Pompeii.

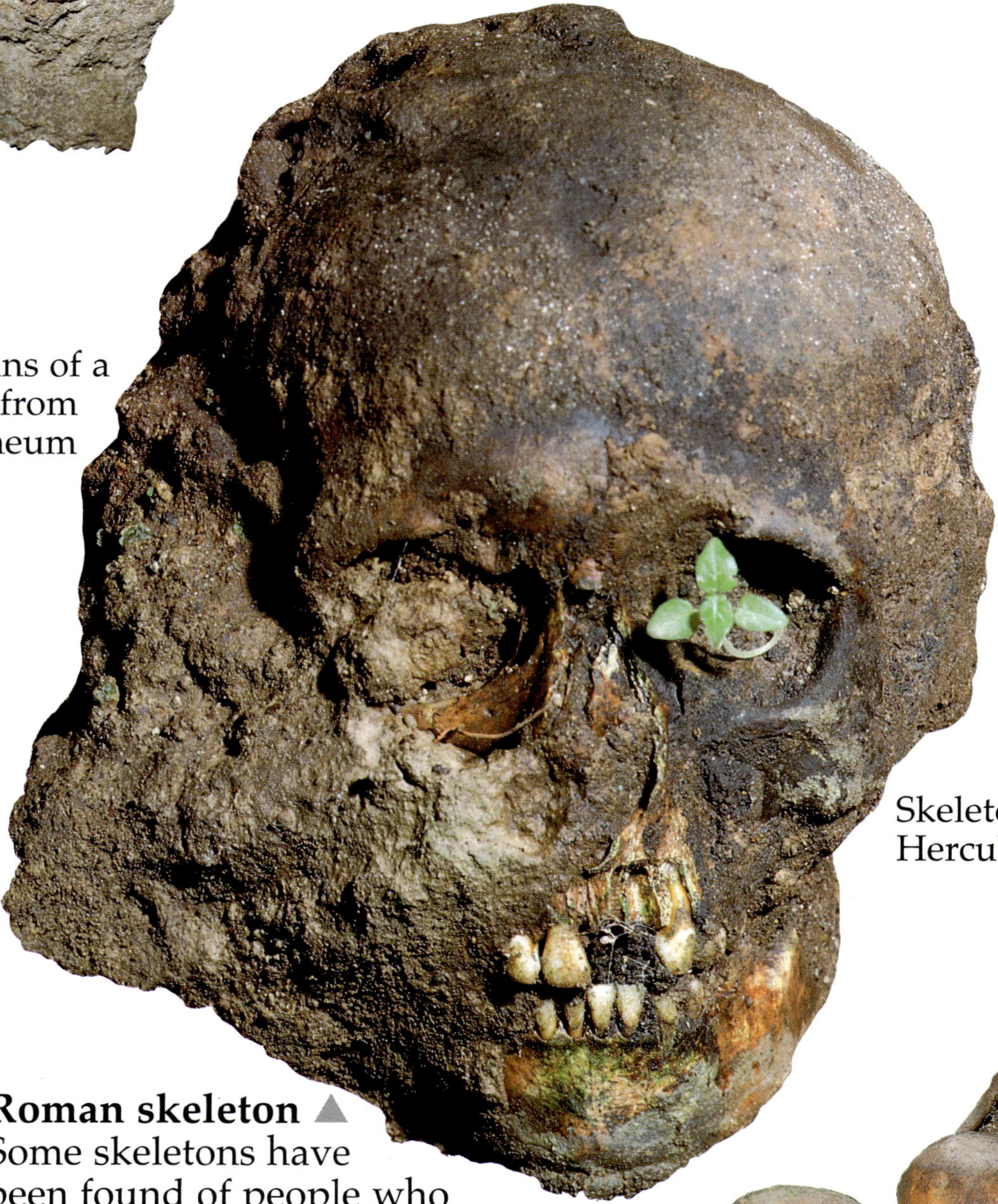

Roman skeleton ▲
Some skeletons have been found of people who died at Herculaneum. Their bodies lay in wet ground, which did not preserve the body shapes.

◀ The ash and rock that covered Herculaneum was about 20 metres thick.

Skeletons found in Herculaneum ▼

▲ 1760

These pictures show Vesuvius erupting.

◀ 1631

▲ 1779

▲ **Surprise eruption**
When Vesuvius exploded in AD 79, it was the first eruption for 800 years! No wonder the people of Pompeii and Herculaneum were taken by surprise. Since then it has erupted many times and it is still active today.

▲ 1885

Tourists on Vesuvius ▶
Since the 1700s, tourists have been visiting Vesuvius. This cartoon shows English tourists in 1890.

▲ Tourists watching the 1933 eruption of Vesuvius.

◀ Tourists can buy boxes of lava and ash to remind them of their visit.

Mount Pelée

Mount Pelée is a volcano on the island of Martinique, in the Caribbean. On the morning of 8 May 1902, Mount Pelée suddenly erupted, sending out a huge glowing avalanche. This cloud of hot gas swept over the nearby city of St Pierre. Within minutes, it had burned down the city and killed 29,000 people. Only two people survived.

▲ The heat damaged the surface of this marble statue.

A broken statue ▲

▲ This watch melted and stopped at quarter past eight.

A melted medicine bottle ▼

Alfred ▶ Lacroix was a scientist. He went to Martinique after the disaster to study glowing avalanches.

Burnt spaghetti

Burnt prune

▼ The remains of a mousetrap

A melted wine bottle

▲ A melted metal fork

Melting heat
All these objects come from the ruins of St Pierre. They were melted by the hot gas.

▲ Human bone

▲ The remains of St Pierre after the eruption. Only a few walls are still standing.

▲ The head of an angel, made from metal

▲ A heap of melted glass

◀ A charred mug

▲ Squashed candlestick

Burnt coffee beans

▲ Charred plate

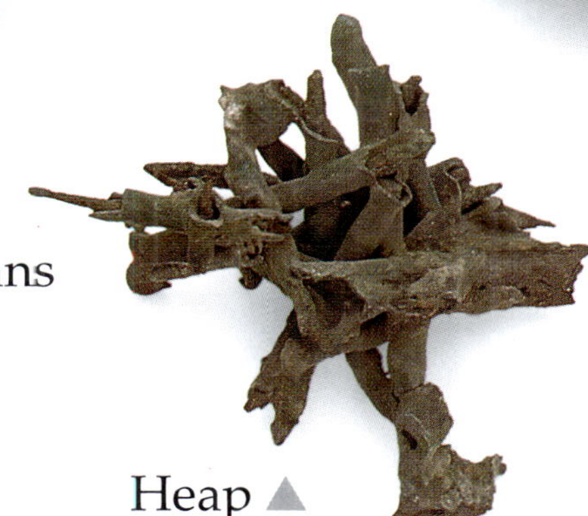

Heap ▲ of iron nails

Melting metal

The gas was hot enough to melt metal. However, the squashed candlestick did not melt. A wall probably fell on it!

▲ Melted metal spoon

The wooden cross was burned off the back of this metal crucifix. ▶

Coins ▶

▲ A prisoner survived the eruption, saved by the walls of his cell. He went on to become a circus star.

Volcanoes and the weather

A big eruption with lots of ash can change the weather. Near the volcano there are strong winds, heavy rain and little sunlight. If the cloud of ash goes high into the sky, it can drift a long way. This can affect the weather all over the world.

▲ **Early Earth**
About 4,000 million years ago, volcanoes covered the Earth. Eruptions formed the planet that we know today.

▲ In 1783, two big eruptions, in Japan and Iceland, caused several very cold winters in Europe and America.

Dinosaur killer? ▼
The dinosaurs may have died from cold caused by volcanic ash and dust blocking out the sunlight.

▼ This dramatic sunset was caused by dust in the air after the eruption of Mount St Helens in 1980.

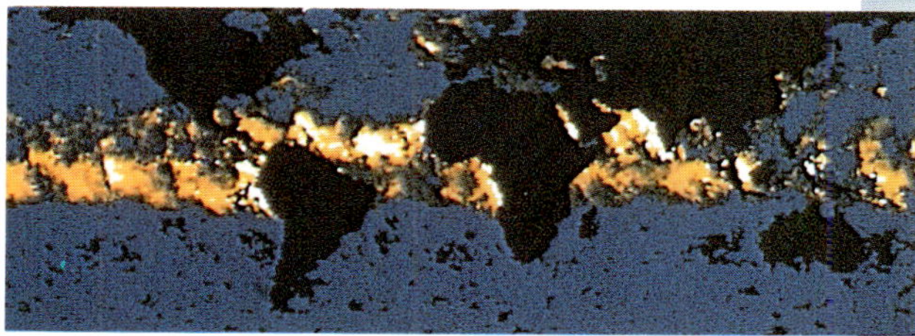

▲ On this map the yellow areas show gas and ash from Mount Pinatubo in 1991. A month after the eruption, the ash had spread all around the world.

▲ The ash cloud from Mount Pinatubo

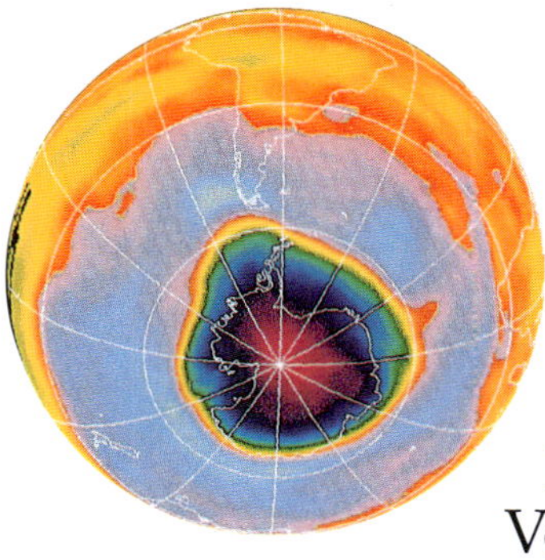

◄ **Ozone hole**
The pink area on this satellite picture is a hole in the protective ozone layer over Antarctica. Volcanic gases could make the hole bigger.

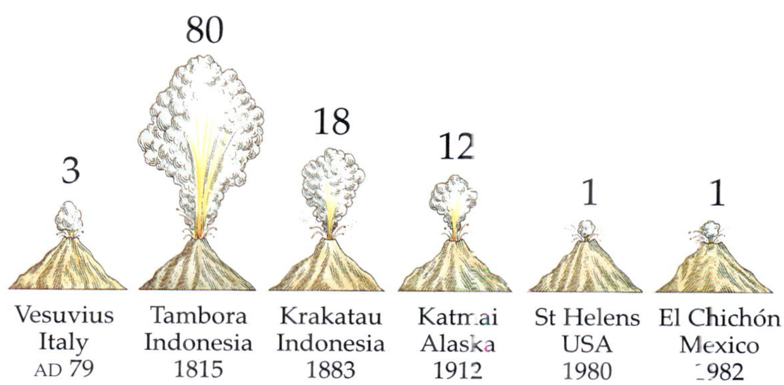

▲ One way to compare eruptions is to work out how much ash a volcano gives out. This diagram shows these amounts in cubic kilometres.

▲ **Pumice from Krakatau**
In 1883, a huge eruption blew the island of Krakatau in Indonesia to pieces. For months afterwards, floating islands of pumice covered the Indian Ocean.

A painting of Krakatau erupting in 1883 ►

Fumaroles and geysers

Where volcanic heat warms an area of ground, water in the ground gets hot too. Steam from this hot water escapes through holes called fumaroles. In some places, hot water shoots out of holes in the ground in fountains, called geysers. In other places pools of bubbling mud are formed.

▲ Vulcan was the ancient Roman god of fire. This picture shows him at work in his blacksmith's forge.

Thermocouple

◀ **Measuring the heat** Scientists use a special electric thermometer, called a thermocouple, to measure heat coming from fumaroles. They can get clues about future eruptions by measuring this heat.

▲ Volcanic gases often contain sulphur (see page 20). As the gases cool, the sulphur hardens into yellow crystals. These large crystals are from Sicily in Italy.

◀ **Healthy steam** Many people visit Solfatara in Italy for their health. They think that the steam and gases from fumaroles are good for their skin and joints.

◀ **Bubbling mud**
Sometimes the rocks around a fumarole melt into mud. The steam bubbles up through the mud, making strange plopping noises.

◀ You can see spiky growths of sulphur around this fumarole.

▲ The ancient Romans built large public baths in places with hot water springs.

Lava covered with sulphur crystals ▼

This plate shows the Old Faithful geyser in the USA. ▶

◀ **Water power**
In some places, people use hot water from the ground to heat buildings and make electricity. This is called hydrothermal energy.

Dormant volcanoes

If a volcano is still active, but it has not erupted for some time, it is called dormant. Below the volcano, the magma is cooling down. As it cools, gases rise up through the rocks. These gases form new, colourful minerals and crystals in the rocks.

▲ A church built on the remains of an old volcano in France

Zeolite crystals ▲

◀ Zeolite crystals grow in the spaces left by old gas bubbles in lava.

This ▶ beautiful layered rock is an agate. The outer layers are older than the crystals in the middle.

▲ Exploring Hekla, a volcano in Iceland

Crater lake ▶ Some volcanoes have craters, or holes, which fill with rainwater. These are called crater lakes.

◀ Brightly coloured rocks at Solfatara in Italy

▲ Olivine is a green volcanic rock.

Cut diamond ▶ 

Gemstones

Sometimes volcanic liquids get trapped in hollows in the rock. They cool down and form large crystals. These crystals can be cut and polished to make gemstones.

▲ An uncut diamond in volcanic rock

Peridot ▶ is the gem made from olivine.

▲ An agate from Brazil

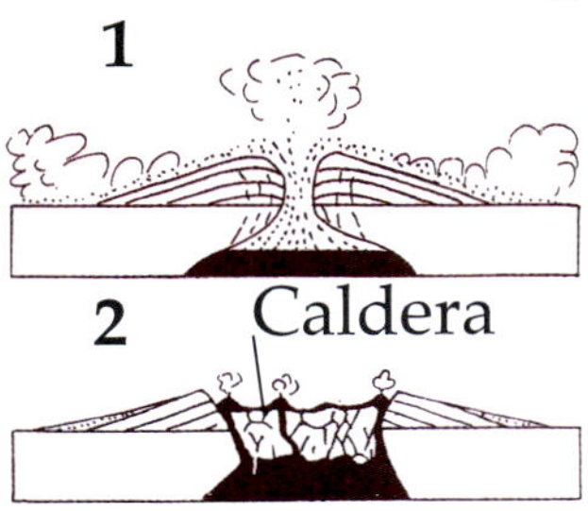

◀ **Caldera**
In a large eruption, the volcano walls may collapse. This forms a large crater called a caldera.

◀ The Greek islands of Santorini are actually the top edges of a large caldera. The caldera itself is full of seawater.

▲ **Cascade volcano**
Mount Rainier is a dormant volcano in the Cascade mountains in the USA. It could become active again one day.

Life on the lava

1 The 1944 lava flow on Mount Vesuvius

▲ Lava

If a volcano spreads a thin covering of ash over the land, it is good news for farmers because ash helps to fertilize the soil. But thick flows of lava are bad news. The lava destroys everything it touches and it can take years for plants to grow back again.

▲ A fern has taken root on lava that is less than one year old.

2 Lichens are often the first plants to grow.

Starting to grow
These pieces of lava are all from the same lava flow on Mount Vesuvius. They show how plants start to grow on lava after an eruption.

3 Lichens eventually cover the lava.

4 When the lava breaks down to make soil, grass starts to grow.

5 Eventually the soil is thick enough for larger plants to grow.

Mount Vesuvius ▶
Mount Vesuvius after a small eruption. There are no plants growing on the slopes.

▲ In 1963, the island of Surtsey was formed by a volcanic eruption.

▲ Seeds were carried to Surtsey by the wind and sea, and plants began to grow on the ash.

▲ **Fertile soil**
Plants like grapes grow well in the soil around Vesuvius because it is fertilized by volcanic ash.

Volcanic wine ▶
There are many vineyards on the slopes of Mount Vesuvius in Italy.

6 This shrub was one of the first large plants to grow on the lava.

▲ Many wine and oil jars were found at Pompeii in Italy. They show that the soil was fertile in Roman times.

Venus, ▶ the Roman goddess of fertility

Volcanologists

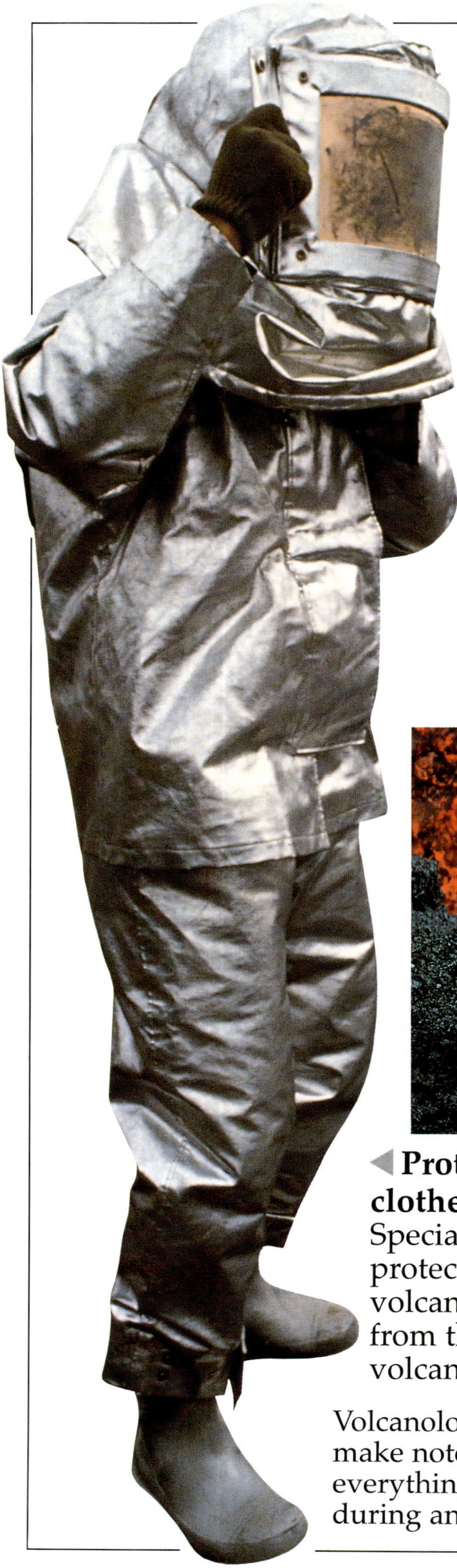

Scientists who study volcanoes are called volcanologists. They spend years watching volcanoes, trying to work out when they will next erupt. Most of the time they work in offices but sometimes they go out to active, or erupting, volcanoes. They collect samples of lava, and measure changes in temperature and the movement of the land.

◀ Katia Krafft spent her whole life studying volcanoes.

◀ **Protective clothes**
Special clothing protects volcanologists from the volcano's heat.

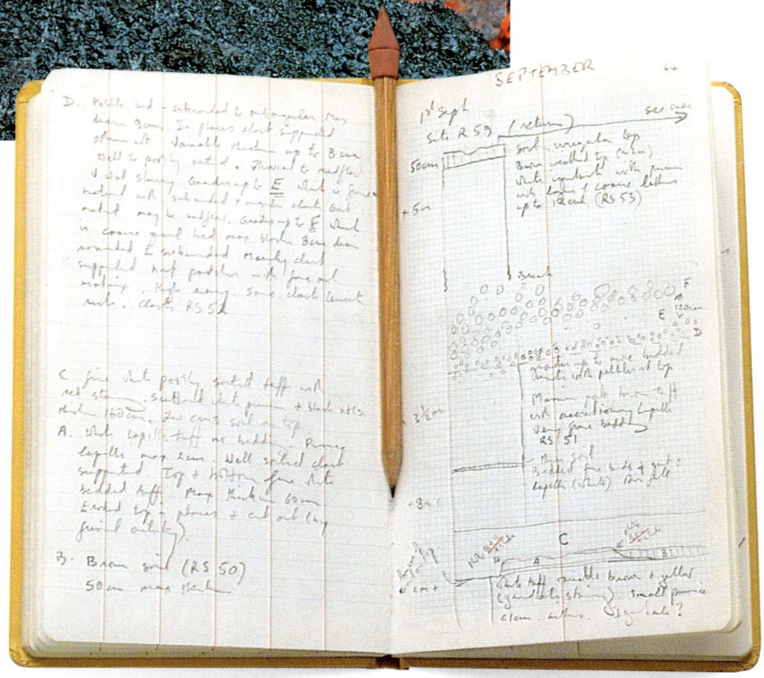

Volcanologists ▶ make notes about everything they see during an eruption.

◀ This metal rod is used to collect blobs of red-hot lava.

▲ Hard hats and special gloves help to protect volcanologists.

▲ Tape measure for measuring cracks in the ground

▲ Binoculars let people watch an eruption from a safe distance.

◀ Instrument for mapping new land during an eruption

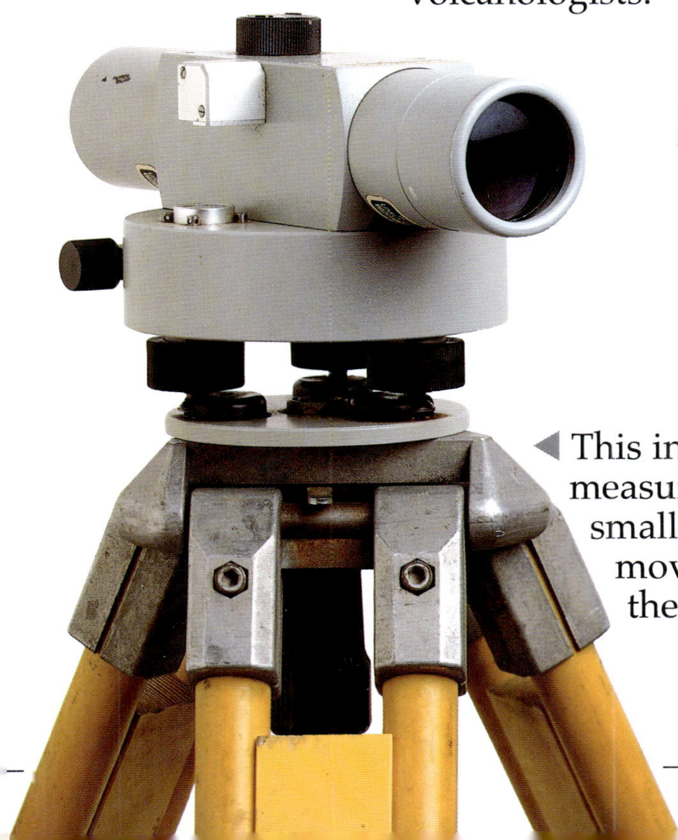

◀ This instrument measures the smallest movements of the ground.

Thermometer that ▶ measures up to 250°C

▲ **Taking the temperature** Katia Krafft uses a thermometer called a thermocouple to take the temperature of the lava.

On other planets

Many spacecraft have been sent into the Solar System to study other moons and planets. They have brought back photos and even pieces of rock. From studying these, we know that the Moon and Mars have volcanoes that have been dead for millions of years. Only Io, one of the planet Jupiter's 16 moons, has volcanoes that are still erupting today.

◀ *The Little Prince* is a story about a prince who lived on a planet in space. The planet had two active volcanoes and one extinct volcano.

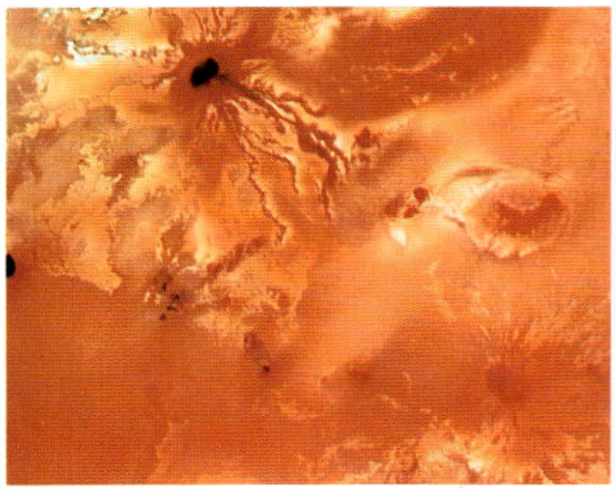

The two Voyager ▲ spacecraft flew past Io in 1979 and photographed Io's colourful surface.

Olympus Mons ▶ This extinct volcano on the planet Mars is the largest volcano found in the universe to date. It is 25 kilometres high!

▲ The spacecraft Magellan took this picture of the planet Venus. Both the volcanoes are dormant.

Erupting in space ▶ In this picture of Io, the volcano Prometheus is erupting. It has thrown up a huge cloud of gas.

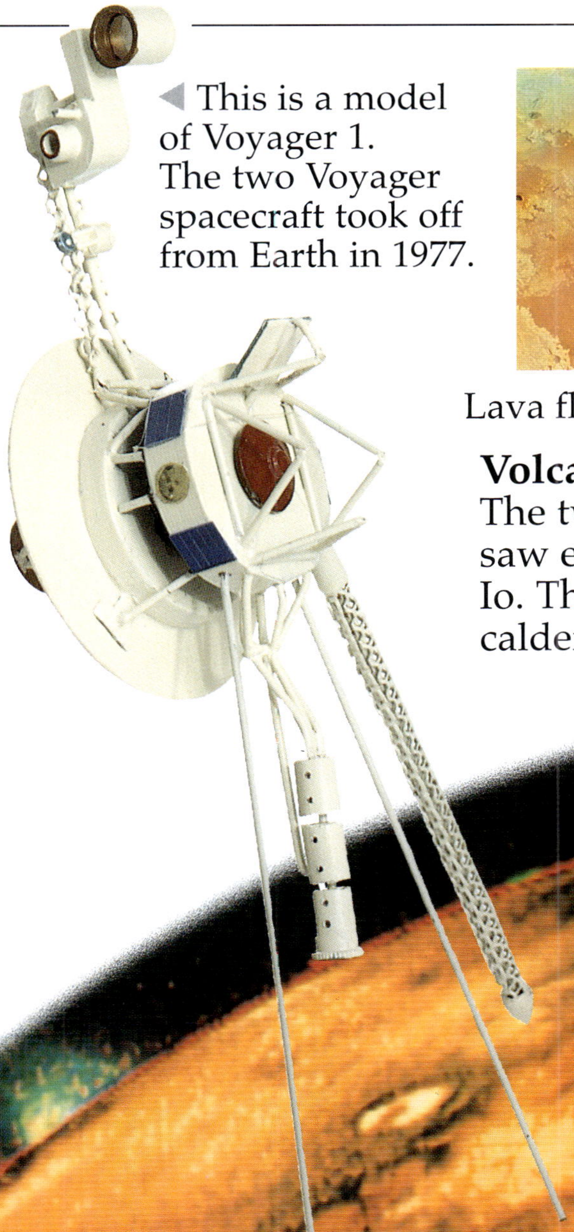

◀ This is a model of Voyager 1. The two Voyager spacecraft took off from Earth in 1977.

Volcanoes on Io ▲
The two Voyagers saw eight erupting volcanoes on Io. They also photographed huge calderas full of molten lava.

Earthquake!

▲ A cartoon of the Earth after an earthquake.

Most earthquakes last less than one minute. But in that short time, the shaking can destroy homes, shops, and even whole cities. Afterwards there are often huge cracks in the ground. An earthquake is a terrifying experience.

▼ **Collapsed buildings** These wooden buildings in San Francisco, USA collapsed during an earthquake in 1989.

▲ A film about an earthquake in Los Angeles, USA

▲ People rush into the streets during an earthquake in Valparaiso, Chile in 1906.

Folded ▶ This book was found in the ruins of a building after an earthquake in Skopje, Yugoslavia in 1963.

▲ A picture from a house in Pompeii, Italy. It shows buildings damaged by an earthquake.

▲ In severe earthquakes, roads crack and crumble.

◀ The Roman author, Seneca, wrote about the earthquake at Pompeii, Italy in AD 62.

▲ Volcanic eruptions can also make the earth shake. These movements are called tremors.

▲ This piece of limestone rock broke in two during an earthquake.

The French writer, ▶ Voltaire, included the Lisbon earthquake of 1755 in his novel *Candide.*

▼ Lisbon, 1755

In 1755, a huge earthquake destroyed three-quarters of the buildings in Lisbon, Portugal.

Measuring earthquakes

How do you measure the size of an earthquake? One way is to measure how much the ground moves with an instrument called a seismograph. Scientists can also measure the strength of an earthquake by asking people to fill in questionnaires and by studying buildings that have been affected.

Mercalli's scale
Giuseppe Mercalli was an Italian volcanologist. He wrote a scale with 12 different grades to describe the effects and intensity of an earthquake.

Giuseppe Mercalli (1850-1914)

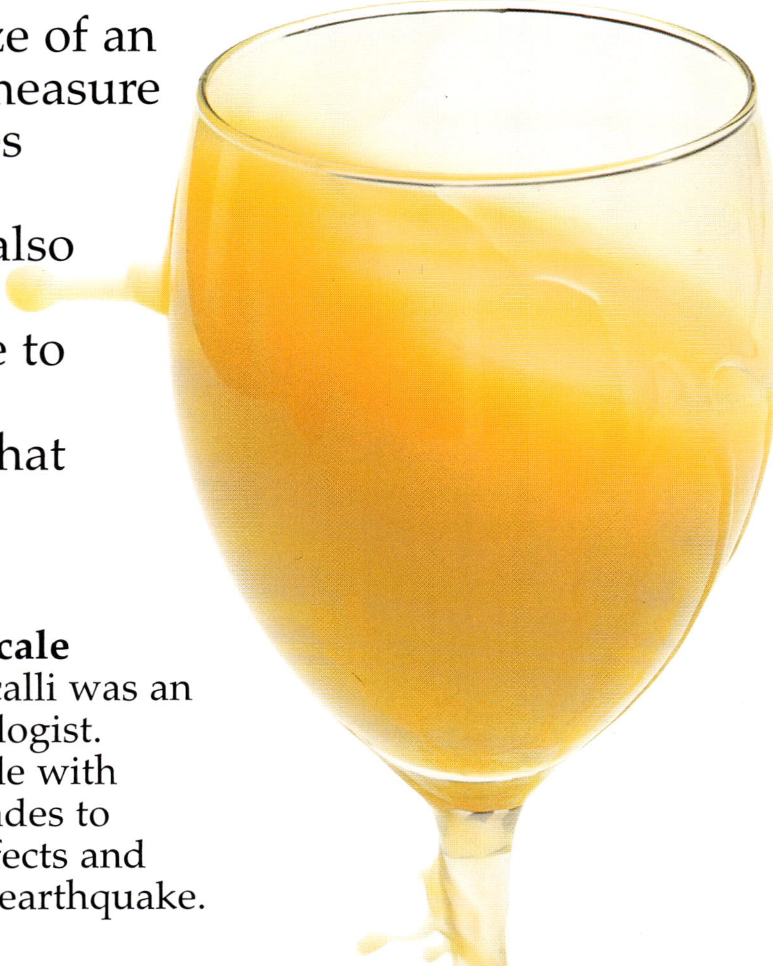

1 Shaking not felt by people.

2 People at rest notice shaking.

3 Hanging objects such as lights swing.

4 Dishes rattle and cars rock.

5 Liquid slops out of glasses.

6 Shaking felt by all. Windows break.

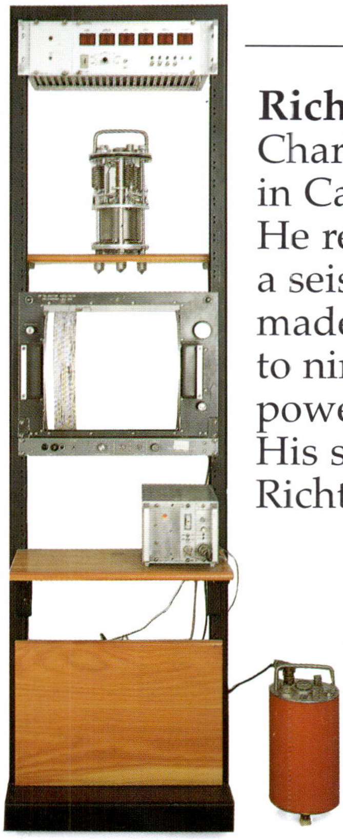

Richter's scale ▶
Charles Richter worked in California in the 1930s. He recorded shakings on a seismograph and then made a scale from zero to nine to describe the power of an earthquake. His scale is called the Richter scale.

Charles F. Richter (1900-1985)

▲ Nowadays instruments can pick up much smaller earthquakes than the ones Richter was able to measure.

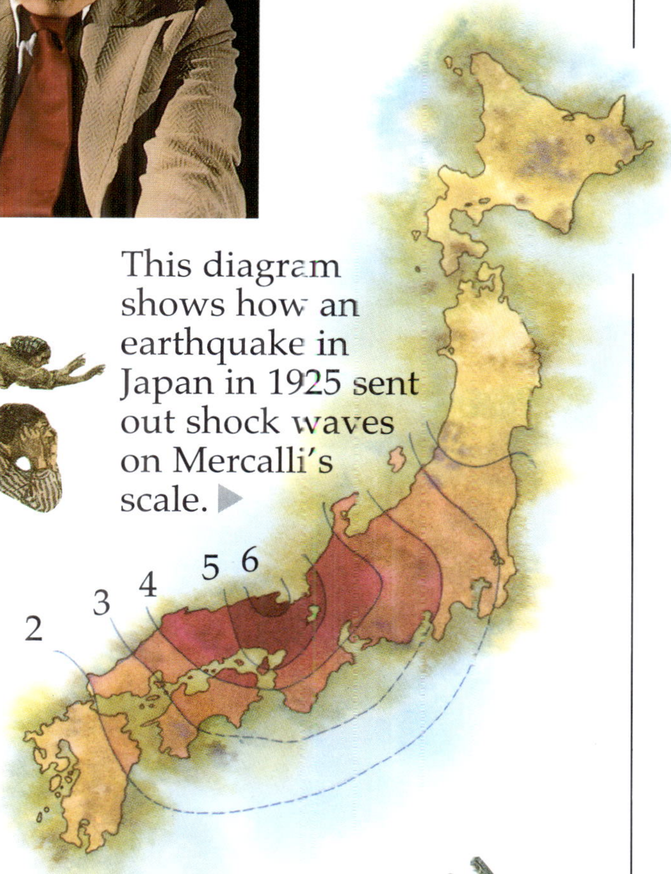

This diagram shows how an earthquake in Japan in 1925 sent out shock waves on Mercalli's scale. ▶

7 It is difficult to stand up.

8 Chimneys and steeples fall down. Cracks in ground.

9 General panic. Some buildings collapse.

10 Water thrown out of rivers. Many buildings collapse.

11 Large cracks appear in the ground. Railway lines break.

12 All buildings destroyed. Ground completely changed.

Earthquake waves

During an earthquake, rocks shatter and break deep below the Earth's surface. This makes shock waves travel through the ground in all directions.
The place on the surface of the Earth directly above the broken rocks is called the epicentre. This is usually where there is most damage. However, the shock waves can travel a long way from the epicentre.

▼ Seismogram

A seismograph makes a drawing of the shock waves of an earthquake. The drawing is called a seismogram.

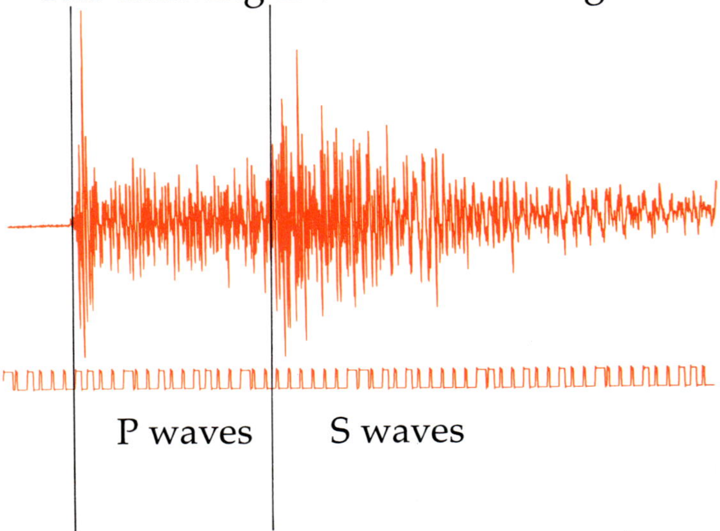

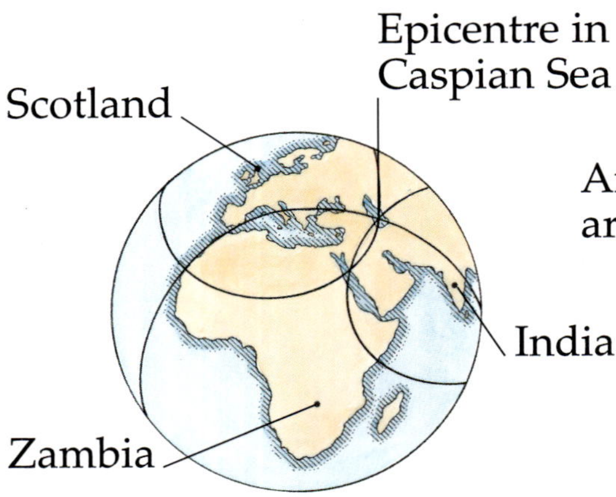

▲ Scientists in India, Zambia and Scotland recorded shock waves in 1989. The earthquake's epicentre was in the Caspian Sea.

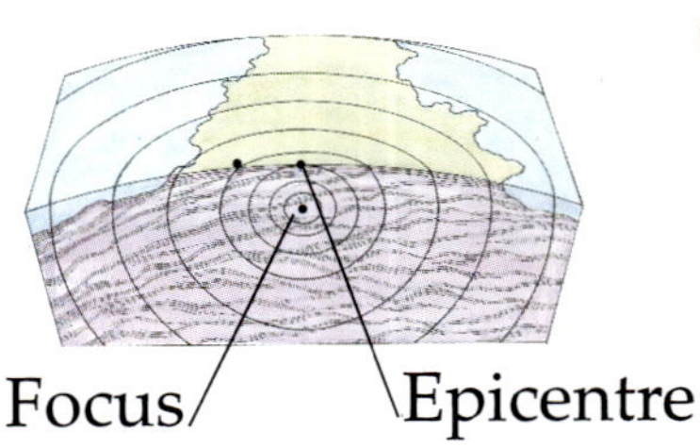

▲ The place where rocks move or break is called the focus of an earthquake. It is deep inside the Earth.

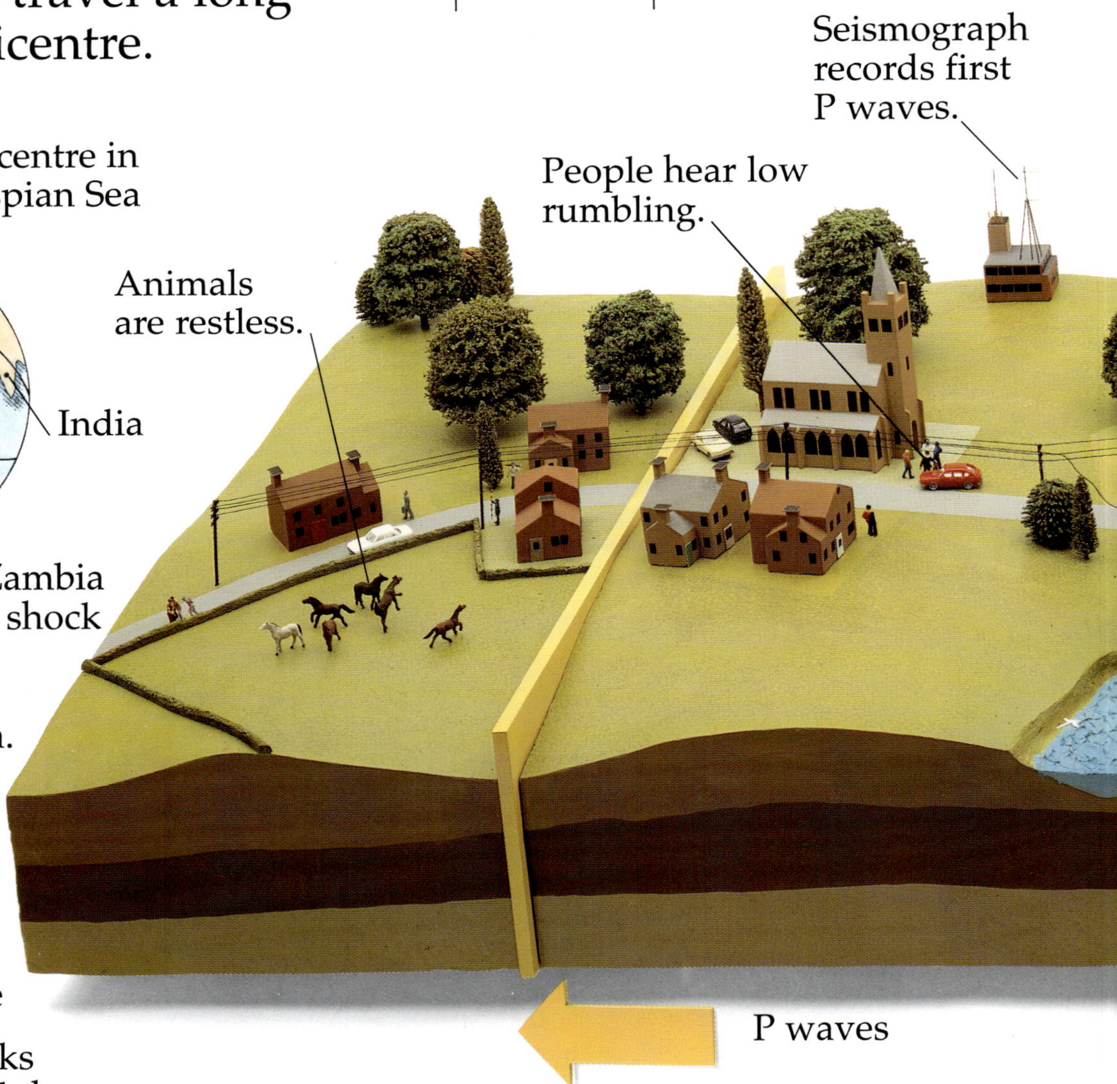

▲ The first waves are called Primary (P) waves. They are the fastest waves.

▲ **Pointe-a-Pitre**
In 1843 an earthquake struck the town of Pointe-a-Pitre on the Caribbean island of Guadeloupe. The shaking only lasted for a minute but it destroyed the town.

▲ A woman sits by her ruined house after an earthquake in Turkey.

▼ **Shock waves**
This model shows how the three kinds of shock waves travel through the ground after an earthquake. The earthquake's epicentre is far off the page to the right.

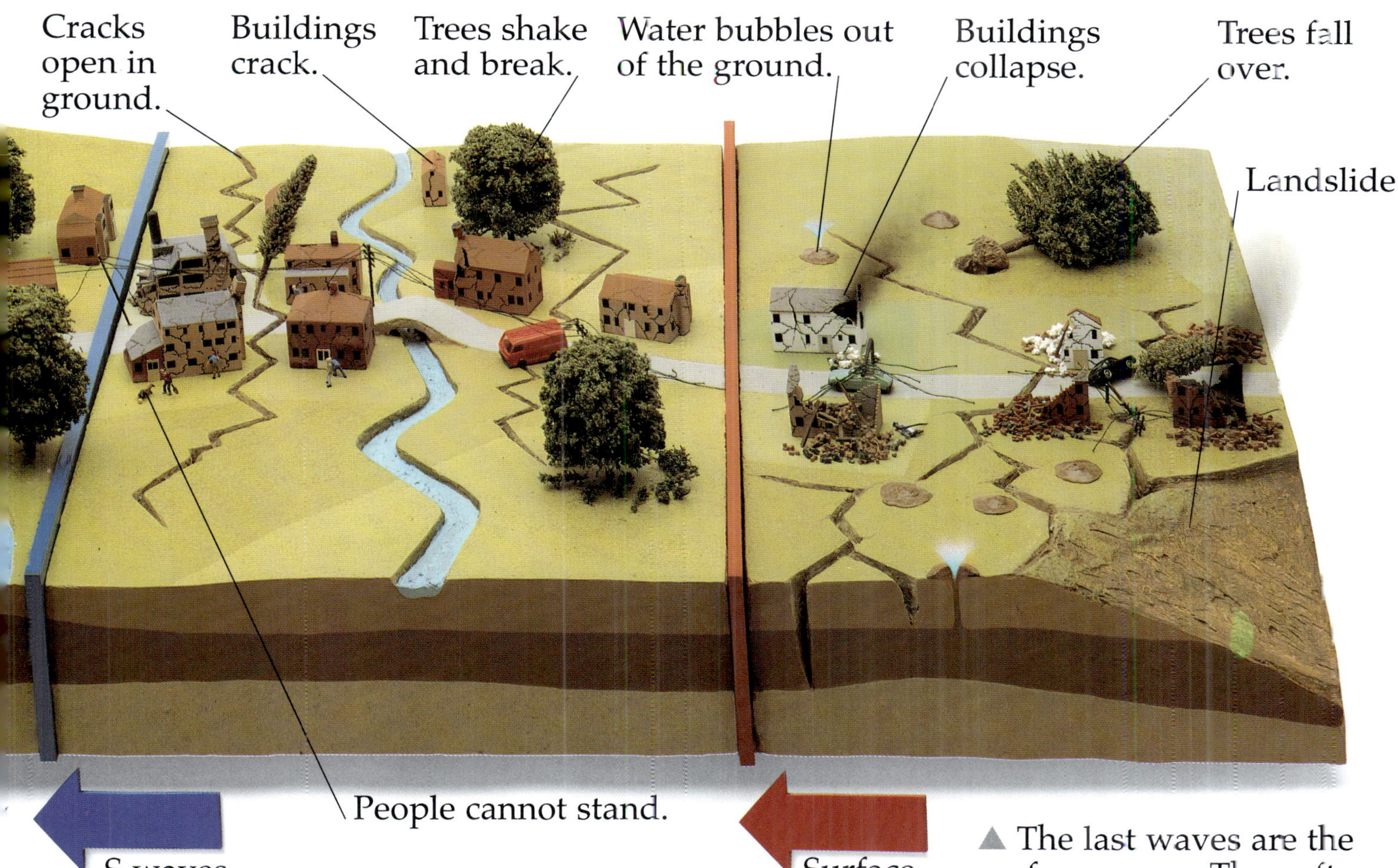

▲ Secondary (S) waves travel more slowly than P waves.

▲ The last waves are the surface waves. They often cause damage far away from the epicentre.

Measuring earthquake waves

▲ Statue of Zhang Heng

In 132, a Chinese scientist called Zhang Heng made the first device for detecting earthquake waves. The instrument could detect even a slight earthquake and tell from which direction it had come. In 1856, an Italian scientist, Luigi Palmieri, made a more complicated earthquake recorder. This was the first seismograph.

▲ Inside the earthquake detector

▼ **Earthquake detector**
This is Zhang Heng's instrument. During an earthquake, the balls drop out of the dragons' mouths into the toads' open mouths.

Ball in dragon's mouth

Open mouth of toad

Clock starts when ground shakes.

Bells

Clockmaker This earthquake instrument was built by Italian clockmaker, Ascanio Filomarino, in 1795. When the ground shook, the bells rang and the clock started to tick.

Ticker tape

This is part of Palmieri's seismograph. It prints a record of the earthquake on ticker tape.

Palmieri's seismograph This seismograph has two parts. One part detects earthquakes, the other part prints out a record of the shaking.

Pendulum records direction of waves.

Spring moves with shock waves.

The observatory where Palmieri worked, near Vesuvius

Luigi Palmieri (1807-1896). His seismograph was the first to use electricity.

◀ In 1923, a huge earthquake destroyed the city of Tokyo in Japan.

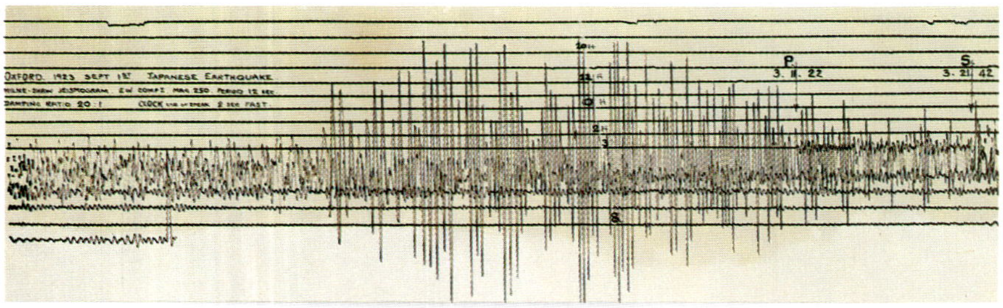

◀ The record of the Tokyo earthquake, drawn by a seismometer.

▲ John Milne was an English geologist who worked in Japan.

Seismometers

All seismometers use pendulums to record the ground shaking.

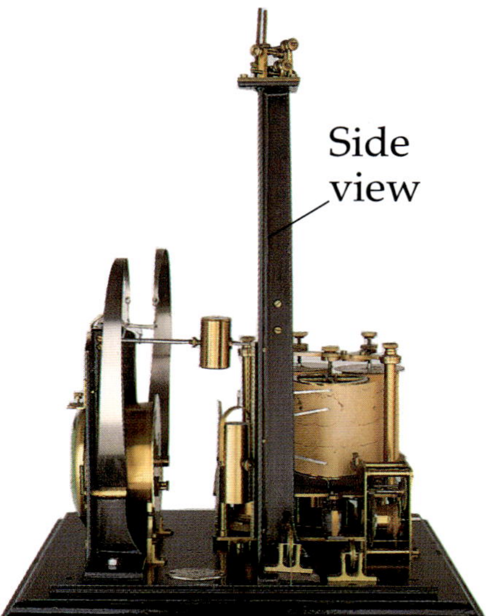

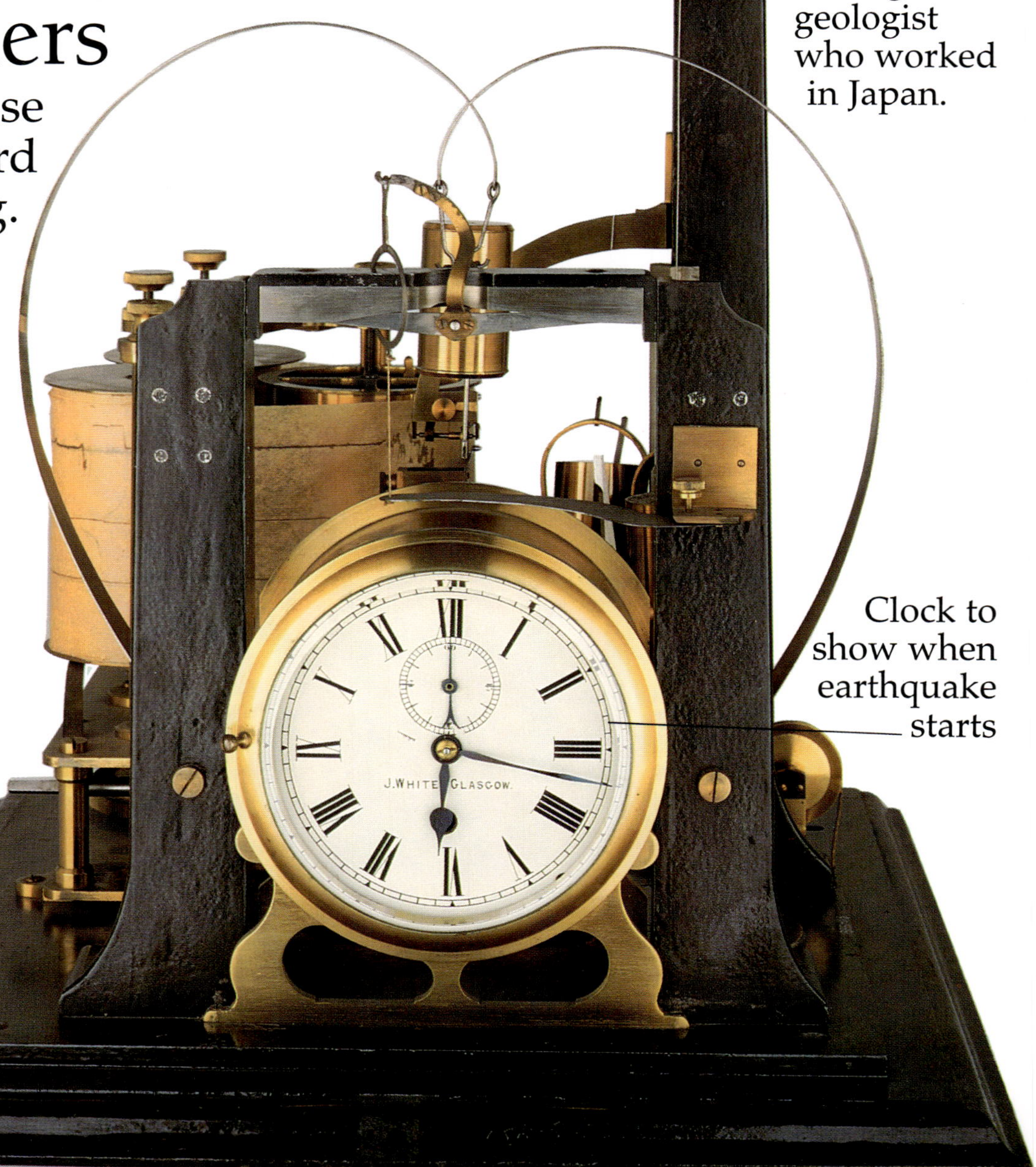

Non-stop use ▶
In 1885, John Milne and Thomas Gray designed this seismometer. It was the first that could be used non-stop.

Earthquake station
This is the modern earthquake station near Mount Vesuvius, in Italy. The rolls of paper are used to record the movements of the ground.

Small seismometers like this one are used outside.

Astronauts left a seismometer on the Moon, to record any moonquakes!

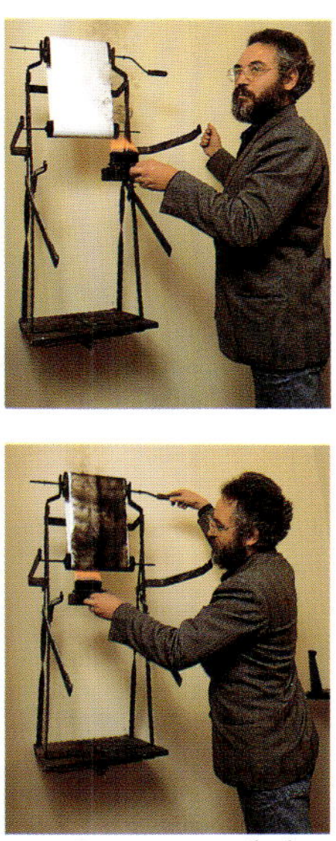

Some old seismometers are still in use. They scratch seismograms on paper made black by smoke.

Hanging pendulums
This large seismometer has heavy hanging pendulums. It was invented in 1908 by Emil Wiechert, a German seismologist.

▲ After the eruption of Mount Pinatubo, in the Philippines (see page 17), huge mud flows destroyed roads, buildings, and bridges.

Mud, floods, and avalanches

Both earthquakes and volcanic eruptions can start avalanches and cause huge ocean waves, called tsunamis. The ash from a volcano can pile up near the crater. If the heap of ash collapses, it will pour down the side of the volcano. And if it rains, this landslide will turn into a river of mud.

◀ **Buried in mud**
In 1985, a river of ashy mud from an erupting volcano killed 22,000 people in the town of Armero in Colombia.

▼ Truck trapped in the mud in Armero, Colombia.

New harbour

Old harbour

◀ Magma from small earthquakes has made the town of Pozzuoli, Italy rise so much that a new harbour has had to be built, lower down.

▲ A picture of a tsunami by a Japanese artist.

Alaska 1964 ▶ One of the longest earthquakes happened in Alaska, USA. It lasted for four minutes. The ground sank and cliffs slid into the sea.

▲ The eruption of Krakatoa (see page 35) caused tsunamis up to 30 metres high.

▲ **Fires after earthquakes** Firefighters put out a blaze after an earthquake in San Francisco, USA in 1989. The shaking often breaks gas pipes, which can cause fires.

Avalanche ▶ In 1970, an earthquake in Peru started a big avalanche. It killed 50,000 people in the valley below.

To the rescue

Rescuing people after an earthquake or a volcanic eruption is difficult and dangerous. Roads are damaged, telephone lines are down, and there is the danger of fire. People are often trapped in damaged buildings which can collapse on the rescuers.

▲ A helicopter lifts a survivor to safety.

A rescuer carries ▶ a man to safety from a mud flow at Armero, Colombia.

Viewer detects the body heat given off by survivors.

Strap worn around the neck

Detecting heat ▲
Rescuers often use a thermal image camera to find people who are trapped in buildings. It detects body heat.

Using a thermal image camera to ▲ search for survivors in the ruins

Vibrations ▶ This machine finds trapped people by picking up vibrations.

A boy is ▶ rescued from the ruins of his home.

▲ Putting out fires after the Mexico City earthquake in 1985

Sniffer dogs ▶ Dogs are used to sniff out people trapped in a fallen building. People can often survive for many days before they are rescued.

Preparing for disasters

People cannot prevent earthquakes and volcanic eruptions. But by planning carefully we can ensure that as few people as possible are killed or injured by these natural events.

▲ Magazines giving tips on how to cope with disasters.

▼ **Safe buildings**
Many buildings in San Francisco, USA are specially designed to stay standing during the shaking of an earthquake.

▲ Over two million people live near Mount Vesuvius in Italy. The volcano is still active today.

▲ Frank Lloyd Wright was one of the first architects to design "earthquake-resistant" buildings.

▼ A machine called a shaking table tests models of buildings to make sure they will stay up in an earthquake. This is an old Japanese shaking table.

◀ **Measuring system**
The red laser beam in this picture is part of a measuring system used in California, USA. It detects how much the ground is moving along the San Andreas fault.

▲ This man has been measuring creep – very slow movement along a fault line.

◀ Scientists study large earthquakes in the past to try to work out when earthquakes are likely to happen in the future.

City rescue ▶ workers practise what to do after an earthquake. The "injured people" are actors.

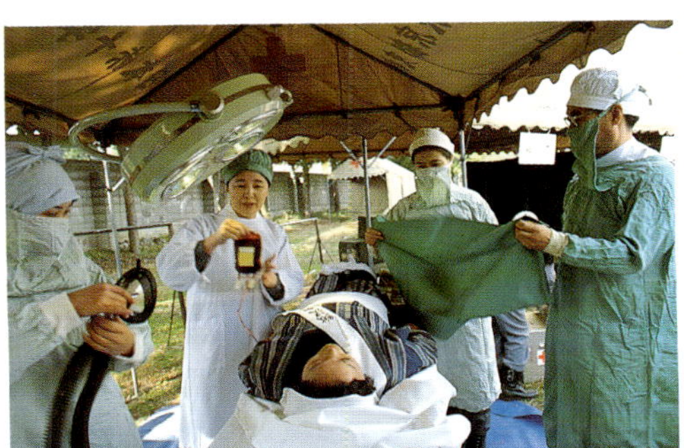

▲ Earthquake rescue practice in Japan.

Earthquake drill ▶
People in Japan and California, USA are taught what to do in an earthquake. The safest places indoors are in a doorway, or under a solid table.

Myths and legends

There are many stories that try to explain why volcanic eruptions and earthquakes happen. In some parts of the world, these stories have been handed on from parents to children for hundreds of years. Today, we call them myths and legends.

◀ A painting of Christians in 1906 trying to stop Vesuvius erupting.

▼ In Central America, people used to throw girls into a lava lake at Masaya to try to stop the volcano erupting.

▼ **Angry gods**
The Aztec people from Mexico believed that the volcano Popocatépetl erupted because the gods were angry. This is an Aztec picture of Popocatépetl.

Giant frog ▶
People in Mongolia thought that the Earth rested on the back of a giant frog. When the frog stumbled, the ground shook with an earthquake.

◀ From above, volcano craters look like giant eyes. This may explain the Greek myth about the Cyclops, a tribe of one-eyed giants who hurled fire and rocks when they were angry.

The Greek sea god was ▼ Poseidon. When he was angry, he banged the sea floor with his trident. This caused earthquakes.

In the Bible, God ▶ destroyed the cities of Sodom and Gomorrah with flood and fire.

The Greeks ▲ believed that the god Hephaistos had his blacksmith's workshops underneath volcanoes.

▲ A Japanese myth says earthquakes are caused by the movements of a giant catfish. Here the gods are flying over a town that has been destroyed by the catfish.

A God's home ▶ Japanese legend says that Mount Fuji is the home of the god Kunitokotache.

Glossary

epicentre – the place on the surface of the Earth directly above the focus of an earthquake.

focus – the place where rocks in the Earth's crust move or break in an earthquake.

fumarole – a hole in the ground in volcanic areas from which steam and gases escape.

geyser – a hot fountain of boiling water which shoots out of the ground in places with volcanic activity.

glowing avalanche – a cloud of ash and gas from an erupting volcano which flows down the side of the volcano.

hot spot – an area where the mantle is very active and makes enough magma to break through the Earth's crust.

hydrothermal energy – energy from hot water and steam heated by volcanic activity.

lava – the red-hot rock that comes out of an erupting volcano.

magma – red-hot, melted rock from the mantle.

mantle – the layer of white-hot, solid rock that lies beneath the Earth's crust.

meterorite – a lump of stone or metal that has fallen to Earth from space.

plate – one of the large pieces that make up the Earth's outer layer.

seismogram – the record of an earthquake made by a seismograph.

seismograph – an instrument used to detect, record and measure an earthquake.

seismologist – a scientist who studies earthquakes.

spreading ridge – an area where two plates are moving apart and new crust is being created.

tsunami – a huge ocean wave caused by the movement of the Earth in an earthquake or volcanic eruption.

volcanologist – a scientist who studies volcanoes.

Index

Acknowledgements

Original version of this book designed and edited by: Scott Steedman, Christian Sévigny, Yael Freudmann, Helen Parker, Julia Harris.
Consultants: Professor John Guest, Dr Robin Adams
Dorling Kindersley would like to thank: John Lepine and Jane Insley of the Science Museum, London; Robert Symes, Colin Keates & Tim Parmenter of the Natural History Museum, London; the staff at the Museo Archeologico di Napoli; Giuseppe Luongo, Luigi Iadicicco & Vincenzo D'Errico at the Vesuvius Observatory for help in photograph-ing the instruments on pp. 49, 53 & 55; Paul Arthur; Paul Cole; Lina Ferrante at Pompeii; Dott. Angarano at Solfatara; Carlo Illario at Hercul-aneum; Roger Musson of the British Geological Survey; Joe Cann; Tina Chambers for extra photography; Gin von Noorden and Helena Spiteri for editorial assistance; Céline Carez for research and development; Wilfred Wood and Earl Neish for design assistance. Illustrations John Woodcock Maps Sallie Alane Reason Models David Donkin (pp. 8–9, 50–51) & Edward Laurence Associates (pp. 12–13)

Picture credits
(Abbreviations; r = Right, l = Left, t = Top, c = Centre, b = Below)
Ancient Art & Architecture Collection: 47t; Art Directors Photo Library: 47tc, 49tc; B.F.I.: 46cr, 57cr; Bridgeman Art Library: 6tl & c; Musee des Beaux-Arts, Lille: 44tl; 44cr; British Museum: 27tr & c; Herge/Casterman: 20tl; Dr Joe Cann, University of Leeds: 25bc; Jean-Loup Charmet: 27bl, 31tl, 46bl, 51tl; Circus World Museum, Baraboo, Wisconsin: 32br; Eric Crichton: 41tr, 41bl; Culver Pictures Inc: 60br; Earthquake Research Institute, University of Tokyo: 63cr; Edimedia/Russian Museum, Leningrad: 28cl; E.T. Archive: 49c, 58tr, 62tl; Mary Evans Picture Library: 8tc, 16tl, 26tl, 27br, 28c, 29cr, 46tl; Le Figaro Magazine/Philippe Bourseiller: 19t, 19cl, 19bl, 19br, 35tr; Fiorepress: 49br; Gallimard: 44tr; G.S.F.: 13tl, 14bl; /Frank Fitch: 20c; John Guest c.NASA: 44bl; Robert Harding Picture Library: 12tl, 14tr, 15cr, 17tr, 17cr, 20tr, 21br, 63br, 24tl, 38br, 39br, 40tr, 42c, 43br, 48br, 49bl, 51tr, 60lc, 62bl, 62-63c; Bruce C. Heezen & Marie Tharp, 1977/c.Marie Tharp: 11c; Historical Pictures Service, Inc.: 10cr; Michael Holford: 22tr; Illustrated London News: 60bl; Frank Lane Picture Agency: 23rct, 23c; Archive Larousse-Giraudon: 32cl; Frank Lane Picture Agency/S.Jonasson: 41tc, 49cr; /S.McCutcheon: 57c; London Fire Brigade/LFCDA: 58bl; Mansell Collection: 31tr; N.A.S.A.: 24bc, 55cr; Natural History Museum: 34tl; National Maritime Museum: 8tl; Orion Press: 7tr, 61bl; Oxford Scientific Films/Kim Westerkov: 11bl; 15tl; Planet Earth Pictures/Franz J.Camenzind: 7cr; /D.Weisel: 17br; /James D. Watt: 23rcb; Robert Hessler: 25tr, 25lc; Popperfoto: 6b, 11tr, 54tl; R.C.S. Rizzoli: 48lc; Gary Rosenquist: 14tl, 14br, 15tr, 15br; Scala: 7c, 49bl(inset); /Louvre: 63tr; Science Photo Library/Earth Sattelite Corp.: 7tl; /Peter Menzel: 7br; /David Parker: 13tr; /Ray Fairbanks: 18c; /Peter Menzel: 20br; /Inst Oceanographic Sciences: 24c; /Matthew Shipp: 24bl; /NASA: 35c, 43cr, 44cr, 44c, 44-45b; /U.S.G.S.: 45tr; /Peter Menzel: 46cl; /Peter Ryan: 55tr; /David Parker: 61tl, 61tr; Frank Spooner Pictures: 8cl, 16cr, 17tl, 22bl, 23tr, 23br, 35tc, 42cl, 47cl, 49cl, 56tl, 56c, 56bl, 57bl, 58tl, 59tr, 59bl, 59br, 61lcb; Syndication International: 31cr; /Inst. Geological Science: 32tc, 35br, 41tl, 47br; /Daily Mirror: 54tr, 57tr; Susanna van Rose: 39bl; Woods Hole Oceano-graphic Institute/Rod Catanach: 24br; /Dudley Foster: 25bl; /J.Frederick Grassle: 25tc; /Robert Hessler: 25tl; ZEFA: 9tl, 21t, 34bl, 45br, 57br.

Every effort has been made to trace the copyright holders and we apologise in advance for any unintentional omissions. We would be pleased to insert the appropriate acknowledgement in any subsequent edition of this publication.